LIBERTY AND COMMUNITY

LIBERTY AND COMMUNITY

THE POLITICAL PHILOSOPHY OF
WILLIAM ERNEST HOCKING

by

Robert Byron Thigpen

Louisiana State University in New Orleans

MARTINUS NIJHOFF / THE HAGUE / 1972

TO
BYRON AND BESS THIGPEN
MY FATHER AND MOTHER

ISBN 90 247 1294 7

PRINTED IN THE NETHERLANDS

PREFACE

This study of the political philosophy of William Ernest Hocking began as a doctoral dissertation at Tulane University. Hocking (1873-1966) was for many years Alford Professor of Natural Religion, Moral Philosophy, and Civil Polity at Harvard University. Although he is relatively well-known among American philosophers, particularly by students of metaphysics and the philosophy of religion, very little attention has been given to his political philosophy. Some general studies of his thought summarize his political writings in a very cursory fashion, but they do not discuss his contributions in detail or relate them to significant issues in political philosophy. Most important general works on modern political philosophy or American political thought do not even mention Hocking; a few note his name in passing. Because he is almost completely unknown in the social sciences, the original purpose of this study was to explore, systematize, and present his extensive writings in political philosophy.

It then became apparent that his entire political philosophy is oriented around the concepts of liberty and community. When his thought is analyzed in terms of these themes, its unity and coherence are more obvious. Moreover, his writings become more significant when they are related to liberty and community, for these are focal concepts for important problems in modern political philosophy. This study of Hocking's political philosophy will, it is hoped, help us to see how liberty and community can be more understandable, attainable, and compatible with one another. This book argues that Hocking's contributions deserve wider consideration by social scientists, political philosophers, and the educated public. And since Hocking's philosophy is an interconnected whole, students of other dimensions of his thought should appreciate a full-length work on his political philosophy.

141251

My debts are extensive; only a few can be acknowledged. Of course, none of the persons mentioned bears any responsibility for this manuscript. Professor René de Visme Williamson of Louisiana State University at Baton Rouge first stimulated my interest in political philosophy. Professors John Schaar and Sheldon Wolin, formerly of the University of California at Berkeley, showed in their teaching and scholarship that no realm of human knowledge is beyond the unifying scope of political theory and that political theory cannot abandon its prophetic role. Professor Jean Danielson of Tulane University originally suggested that I investigate Hocking's political philosophy. Professor Warren Roberts, Jr. of Tulane was a careful, perceptive advisor as chairman of my dissertation committee. More than this, his qualities of mind and character, his thoughtfulness and his concern for students, will be a model for all by teaching.

I have benefited greatly from my many conversations with Professor Lyle A. Downing, my friend and colleague at Louisiana State University in New Orleans. He personally exemplifies these two tenets of Hocking's philosophy: the sharing of ideas in dialogue is central to both our knowledge and our humanity; and theory must begin in experience and receive its justification in its illumination of experience. Professor Richard Hocking, son of William Ernest Hocking, kindly granted me permission to examine his father's unpublished papers in the family library in Madison, New Hampshire. Mrs. Jan Davis was a competent typist and an excellent source of experience concerning manuscript preparation. Finally, my wife, Jo Ann, was patient and encouraging during the travails of authorship. She shouldered more of our family responsibilities than were properly hers.

RBT

New Orleans, Louisiana
August, 1971

CONTENTS

ABBREVIATIONS USED IN THE NOTES

CWC   *The Coming World Civilization*

EE   *Experiment in Education*

FP   *Freedom of the Press*

HNR   *Human Nature and Its Remaking*

LEI   *The Lasting Elements of Individualism*

LRWF   *Living Religions and a World Faith*

MATS   *Man and the State*

MGHE   *The Meaning of God in Human Experience*

MIHE   *The Meaning of Immortality in Human Experience*

PP   *Preface to Philosophy*

PLR   *Present Status of the Philosophy of Law and of Rights*

SIG   *Science and the Idea of God*

SBF   *The Self: Its Body and Freedom*

SMN   *Strength of Men and Nations*

SWP   *The Spirit of World Politics*

TP   *Types of Philosophy*

The Selected Bibliography contains full bibliographical information for cited articles by Hocking.

INTRODUCTION
LIBERTY AND COMMUNITY AS PROBLEMS

Liberty and community have become problematical in contemporary Western society. The experience of both has decreased in the everyday awareness of people. The early modern period began with a high expectation that the liberation of the individual from authorities of all kinds and from close communal bonds would lead to both personal happiness and the full flowering of individual talents. This optimistic assumption has not been realized. Our era has been termed variously as the age of "anxiety," or "insecurity," or "anomie." Kenneth Keniston points out that common words currently used to describe the breakdown of meaningful relationships between men, and between men and the social order, are "alienation, estrangement, separation, withdrawal, indifference, disaffection, apathy, noninvolvement, neutralism."[1] The term most often employed to describe the common experience of vast numbers of people in the western world is "alienation." As Robert A. Nisbet states, "Alienation is one of the determining realities of the contemporary age: not merely a key concept in philosophy, literature, and the social sciences." It is "a cultural and psychological condition implicating ever larger sections of the population."[2] The theme of alienation is so powerful that there is no need to discuss its representations in literature and the arts, in philosophy and social criticism.[3] During the past two decades, there has also been a great deal of writing on "mass society," the social dimension of personal alienation. The concept of "mass society" is often utilized to discuss societies where great numbers of people are not integrated into significant and meaningful social groupings.[4]

[1] "Alienation and the Decline of Utopia," in *Varieties of Modern Social Theory*, ed. by Hendrick M. Ruitenbeek (New York: E. P. Dutton and Co., Inc., 1963), p. 79.

[2] *Community and Power* (New York: Oxford University Press, 1962), p. viii.

[3] For a discussion of different approaches to alienation, see Fritz Pappenheim, *The Alienation of Modern Man* (New York: Monthly Review Press, 1959). Pappenheim's own interpretation of alienation is based on the work of Marx and Tönnies.

[4] For an excellent summary of the literature on mass society, see William Kornhauser, *The Politics of Mass Society* (New York: The Free Press, 1959), especially pp. 21-38.

The experience of alienation has two dimensions: it consists in the loss of a sense of liberty and the absence of a meaningful experience of community. Liberty and community are not easy to define. Modern man has learned that liberty cannot be understood in Hobbes' terms as the mere absence of external restraints. True liberty flows from the experience that one is in touch with his fundamental nature, that he is discovering and developing his potentialities. There are many definitions of community. One sociologist reports that sixteen concepts are utilized in formulating ninety-four different definitions in sociological literature.[5] As Mason Drukman correctly states, community requires at the minimum a sense of "interdependence" that involves "feelings of strength and sufficiency born of the knowledge that the individual is not alone, that he is supported by society at large, and that society accepts him as a useful and legitimate member."[6] Drukman shows that the experience of community cannot be confused with functional interrelationships. A society may be composed of people who perform highly specialized tasks, each of which is very dependent on the others; but unless there are strong fraternal feelings between the members, the experience of community will be limited.[7]

An historical account of the reasons for the decline in the experience of liberty and community is beyond the scope of this study, though some factors are mentioned below in the fourth chapter. Ferdinand Tönnies pointed out in his famous work, *Gemeinschaft und Gesellschaft*,[8] that the urbanization and developing technology of the modern West contributed to a more rational and contractual style of life, in contrast to the traditional group memberships of feudal society. Although the organic communities of pre-modern Europe were rejected as social models, the new rhetoric of liberty belied its loss at the deepest personal levels. Intellectual life came to be dominated by various forms of determinism, causal systems that accounted for human thought and action in terms of impersonal forces alone. Freedom of decision and the unity of the will were denied. These determinisms also helped to destroy the feeling of community. For, as it will be shown, when the individual is interpreted in a deterministic fashion, sociality is obscured. Community requires that interpersonal relationships be

---

[5] George A. Hillery, Jr., *Communal Organizations* (Chicago, Ill.: University of Chicago Press, 1968), p. 3. See also *Community*, ed. by Carl J. Friedrich (New York: The Liberal Arts Press, Inc., 1959).

[6] *Community and Purpose in America* (New York: McGraw-Hill Book Co., 1971), p. 7.

[7] *Ibid.*, pp. 8-9.

[8] For an explication of Tönnies, see Pappenheim, *op. cit.*, pp. 64-78.

spontaneously entered by individuals who believe they are in full command of their creativity and their commitments.

By the nineteenth century, Sheldon Wolin writes, it was accepted as an "article of faith that no creation, no object, no thought, no act could be rightfully called 'mine.' Everything was society's creation."[9] It was assumed that the individual should seek simply to perform his function in the great social machine. In part because of this assumption, growing numbers of people have come to feel that society stifles both genuine personal relationships and opportunities for individuals to express their innermost capacities. Glenn Tinder states that the term "system" is increasingly used to refer "to the great body of rules and arrangements in society which impersonally determine the individual's fate and form of life but which the individual in turn can do little to understand and control."[10]

The social world beyond the hearthstone has come to seem more impersonal and out of control not only because of the determinisms of modern thought, but also because of the increasing alienation of people from the political order. Many now feel that governmental institutions and political participation are irrelevant to their deepest personal needs. As a consequence, the foundations for common action and the purposive direction of social life have been undermined. Tinder correctly writes, "Politics is the collective thought and action of a society. If this is a 'post-political era,' then as communal and historical beings we are condemned to a kind of stupefaction and paralysis."[11]

So many attempts to call the contemporary citizen back to political involvement seem hollow because they are not based on a theoretical investigation of liberty and community and their relationship to the political order. We cannot concentrate only on political programs and strategies if we are to think seriously about the problems of liberty and community. As John Schaar writes, our task is to develop "the theory and institutions of a community in which men can be *both* conscious and individual *and* share the moral bonds and limits of the group."[12] Any conception of the political community must rest on some set of ideas about man, society, and the nature and purpose of political authority. Because our implicit assumptions on these matters are proving inadequate, political philosophy must become a

[9] *Politics and Vision* (Boston: Little, Brown and Co., 1960), p. 362.
[10] *The Crisis of Political Imagination* (New York: Charles Scribner's Sons, Inc., 1964), p. 92.
[11] *Ibid.*, p. 119.
[12] "Legitimacy in the Modern State," in *Power and Community: Dissenting Essays in Political Science*, ed. by Philip Green and Sanford Levinson (New York: Vintage Books, 1970), p. 298.

focal point for inquiry into the problems of liberty and community.

As various writers have commented, American political thinkers have rarely transcended American institutions and presuppositions. American political theory has been curiously unphilosophical; it has generally not risen above the social and political givens to the level of philosophical analysis.[13] It is therefore unusual and important that a fully developed political philosophy formulated by an established American philosopher has been so largely ignored. This is even more surprising when we realize that his thought focuses on the extremely important concepts of liberty and community. The political philosophy of William Ernest Hocking is thus especially worthy of consideration.

HOCKING'S LIFE AND WORK

This study cannot discuss in detail either Hocking's biography or his general philosophy. That task has been admirably accomplished by Leroy Rouner in *Within Human Experience: The Philosophy of William Ernest Hocking*.[14] Hocking's metaphysics and religious philosophy have also been discussed particularly well by A. R. Luther in *Existence as Dialectical Tension*.[15] Although the effects of Hocking's philosophy on other thinkers cannot easily be traced, some sense of its influence may be gained from an examination of Hocking's *Festschrift*, the massive compilation of essays in his honor edited by Rouner.[16] A brief summary of his life and work is nevertheless in order.[17]

Hocking was a child of the American Middle West. The son of a physician and the eldest of five children, he was born in Cleveland, Ohio in 1873. His deeply religious and closely knit family moved to Joliet, Illinois, when he was six years old. After high school he worked at various jobs for four years to save money for college. Although he entered Iowa State College with the intention of becoming a civil

[13] See, for example, Robert McCloskey, "American Political Thought and the Study of Politics," in *Approaches to the Study of Politics*, ed. by Roland Young (Evanston, Ill.: Northwestern University Press, pp. 155-71. For an example of a work that celebrates this characteristic of American political thought, see Daniel Boorstin, *The Genius of American Politics* (Chicago, Ill.: University of Chicago Press, 1953).
[14] (Cambridge, Mass.: Harvard University Press, 1969).
[15] (The Hague, Netherlands: Martinus Nijhoff, 1968).
[16] *Philosophy, Religion, and the Coming World Civilization*, ed. by Leroy S. Rouner (The Hague, Netherlands: Martinus Nijhoff, 1966).
[17] The best secondary sources of biographical information on Hocking have been prepared by Leroy S. Rouner. See *Within Human Experience, op. cit.*, especially pp. 1-12, and *Philosophy, Religion, and the Coming World Civilization, op. cit.*, pp. 5-22. For Hocking's autobiographical reminiscences, see *Varieties of Educational Experience*, I (Mimeographed, 1952) ,pp. 1-18, and II (Mimeographed, 1954), pp. 14-15b.

engineer, his most important experience there was his introduction to the philosophy of William James. Hocking reports that a reading of *Principles of Psychology* "set me wondering whether I could reach the place where William James taught."[18] To save money for Harvard he worked five more years in Davenport, Iowa, first as a teacher of mathematics at a business college and then as the principal of a public elementary school.[19]

Although he planned to study architecture when he entered Harvard, his interest soon shifted to philosophy. Other than James, the professor whom he found most stimulating was Josiah Royce. He spent a year in Germany, where he studied under Husserl, and received his doctorate in 1904. He taught the history and philosophy of religion for two years at Andover Theological Seminary, a period during which he married Agnes Boyle O'Reilly of Boston, and he then accepted a position at the University of California at Berkeley. He reports that his interest in political philosophy began in California when Professor Howison, the chairman of the department, asked him to lead a class in the study of Bosanquet's *Philosophical Theory of the State*.[20] After two years at California and six years at Yale, he was called to Harvard in 1914, largely on the reputation of *The Meaning of God in Human Experience* (1912), his first and still best known book. He served at Harvard, at times as Chairman of the Philosophy Department, until his retirement in 1943. Living in active retirement on his farm in Madison, New Hampshire, he continued to write for publication, even beyond his ninetieth birthday. He died in 1966 at the age of ninety-three.

Although Hocking's bibliography includes over three hundred entries, those books most important to his political philosophy can be

---

[18] *Varieties of Educational Experience*, I, p. 16.

[19] Hocking never lost his interest in early education. Years later, as a Harvard professor, he and his wife Agnes, along with other professors and their wives, started a school for their own children. The classes met at first on the Hocking's porch and were taught by the professors and their wives. They were then moved to permanent quarters with some professional staff. "Shady Hill School" soon became widely respected, with many more applicants than it could accept. See *Varieties of Educational Experience*, I, pp. 19-36, and "Creating a School" (with Agnes Hocking). For a delightful discussion of the school by a former student, see May Sarton, "I knew a Phoenix in My Youth," *The New Yorker*, April 3, 1954, pp. 29-33.

[20] Hocking reports the incident as follows (*Varieties of Educational Experience*, II, p. 15b): "Ethics, he [Howison] said, culminates in the virtue of the political community. 'How would you like to carry a section of more advanced students through a study of Bosanquet's Philosophy of the State?' 'But, Professor Howison, I know nothing about political philosophy.' 'Never pretend to know anything that you don't know, young man; but read ahead of the class, wrestle it out with them, and by the end of the year you will have something in hand.' And since a request from Howison was equivalent to a command, I again became student in order to teach. For thirty-five years, I continued to work over that topic, in order to teach it – though not solely for that purpose."

briefly mentioned.[21] The decade 1918-1928 was a very creative period; he published four books that set the basic outlines of his social and political thought. *Human Nature and Its Remaking* (1918) and *The Self, Its Body and Freedom* (1928) develop his philosophy of freedom, the structure of the human will and its development, and the nature of sociality and social relationships. *Man and the State* (1926) is an original theory of the political community, and *Present Status of the Philosophy of Law and of Rights* (1926) is a philosophical analysis of the nature of law and the grounds for the legitimate claim of rights by citizens. *Types of Philosophy* (1929) was revised in 1959 in collaboration with his son, Professor Richard Hocking. It is still used as a textbook in university philosophy courses. In *The Lasting Elements of Individualism* (1937) he analyzed the crisis that had developed in liberalism.

Hocking's political thought was influenced by wide travel and the observation of different political systems. During the late 1920's he travelled extensively in Egypt, Palestine, and Syria on behalf of the Bureau of International Research at Harvard. In *The Spirit of World Politics: With Special Studies of the Near East* (1932), published on the basis of this travel, he undertook both a general discussion of international relations and an investigation of the nature of British and French rule in that area. He continued his study of non-Western cultures by traveling in India, Burma, China, and Japan in 1931-32 during his service as chairman of the Commission of Appraisal of the Laymen's Foreign Missions Inquiry. The commission's report, *Rethinking Missions*, was jointly authored by the fifteen members, but it bears Hocking's style of thought and expression. His study of these non-Western cultures and the impact on them of Western economic and political power helped him develop his concept of a "world culture" or "world civilization," discussed in *Living Religions and a World Faith* (1940) and *The Coming World Civilization* (1956). He visited Europe at different times throughout the first half of the century, beginning with two trips during his student days, one of which was earned by work on a cattle boat. During World War I he went to the front in France with a detachment of American military engineers. He travelled in Europe during the late 1930's, when he delivered the Hibbert Lectures at Oxford and Cambridge and the Gifford Lectures in Scotland. In 1947-48 he was a visiting professor at the University of Leiden, and he

---

[21] A selected bibliography is appended to this study. For an almost entirely complete bibliography, see Richard Gilman, "The Bibliography of William Ernest Hocking," in *Philosophy, Religion, and the Coming World Civilization, op. cit.*, pp. 469-504.

investigated the attempted "re-education" of Germany by the allied military occupation forces. This study became a central theme of a general work on education, *Experiment in Education: What we can Learn from Teaching Germany* (1954).

During his later years Hocking achieved wide public eminence. Though he had always given many lectures and addresses, he was in even more demand. Throughout World War II he was a member of the Commission on a Just and Durable Peace, set up in 1940 by the Federal Council of the Churches of Christ in America. This commission, chaired by John Foster Dulles, held conferences and published materials. He served also on the Commission on Freedom of the Press, an independent commission composed of such famous persons as Robert M. Hutchins (Chairman), Reinhold Niebuhr, Zechariah Chafee, Harold Lasswell, Charles Merriam, and Arthur Schlesinger. After what Hocking calls three years of steady labor, he published *Freedom of the Press: A Framework of Principle* (1947). He was also often asked to express his thought on concrete political problems in such periodicals as *Life*, the *Saturday Review*, and the *Christian Century*. An examination of his selected bibliography will show the extent of his concerns.

Hocking was therefore a political philosopher who was deeply involved in the political issues of his time. He always insisted that all philosophy must be derived from experience and must help make sense of experience. But he thought that political philosophy is particularly related to concrete human problems, for it focuses on the subject that is at the same time the most practical and the most theoretical of human activities.

Politics is the most practical of the arts. It is most concerned with "hard facts"; for what facts are harder than the facts of human interest and passion? Yet it is, and always has been, the most theoretical. From earlier than historic times it has been conducted on the basis of some theory, theological or other, of authority and the obligation of obedience. [22]

He believed that the extremes of practice and theory meet in politics for several reasons: politics is an immense enterprise, and the larger the enterprise in which men are engaged the more necessary it is to have a general policy; politics affects people more radically than any other practical activity, since it tampers "with their goods, their families and their lives"; and politics requires thought as to the nature

[22] *MATS*, p. ix.

of human "welfare" and the extent to which this welfare "is capable of being realized under human conditions."[23] Hocking's own political philosophy is grounded in his interest in specific problems. But some of his writings are so closely tied to the political issues of a particular place and time that they are entirely unphilosophical. The book *Morale and Its Enemies* (1918) has this character. This study will discuss such topical writings very little. It will center rather on the general theoretical works, for it is his political philosophy that has continuing significance, not his political commentary.

What Rouner writes about Hocking's metaphysics also applies to his political philosophy. Rouner states that Hocking never finally systematized his metaphysics because pressing human problems attracted his involvement.[24] Although Hocking did not completely systematize his political philosophy, it does have an underlying unity. One purpose of this study is to present its inherently systematic nature. This task is facilitated when his thought is focused on the themes of liberty and community. Another reason why he did not completely systematize his political thought is that he developed it dialectically, from encounter with other positions. He always attempted to present as accurately and powerfully as possible the major theoretical alternatives on the question at hand. He therefore gave much attention to developing and defending, not just to stating, the points of view of others. He then sought the synthesis that would be more adequate than any of the initial positions, his own included. In fact, his writing is so dialectical that a word of caution is necessary to any who would read him casually. The reader must carefully distinguish Hocking's conclusions from those positions he at first defends but later in part rejects.

LIBERTY AND COMMUNITY AS THEMES IN HOCKING'S POLITICAL PHILOSOPHY

Hocking believes that modern thought is caught in a dilemma, a "dilemma of modernity." Our thinking is limited by two assumptions, "the subjective certitude of one's own existence, and the objective certitude of a nature whose process lends itself exhaustively to mathematical expression."[25] One side of the dilemma posits a naturalism that is certain only of the objective reality of natural processes, pro-

---

[23] *Ibid.*
[24] *Within Human Experience, op. cit.*, p. 312.
[25] *TP*, p. vi.

cesses that require a complete causal determinism. The other side of the dilemma consists in a subjectivism that is certain only of the existence of the individual ego. It insists that each self is a completely closed universe of experience in isolation from every other self.[26] This subjectivism leads to solipsism, an individualism so extreme that no common human experience or communication is possible. The effects on liberty and community of this dilemma are obvious. One side of the dilemma, the tendency toward determinism, would make liberty impossible, since it rejects genuine purpose or free decision. The other side of the dilemma, the movement toward solipsism, would make community unattainable, because it denies the reality of shared experience. In the various areas of his philosophy, Hocking seeks a way past this dilemma of modern thought. This search was a central concern of his metaphysics. The present study concentrates on the way his political philosophy transcends the dilemma.

Much contemporary inquiry into man, society, and politics is modeled after the scientific method of the physical sciences. In fact, this is the dominant method now utilized in the social sciences. It has become almost the paradigm for our understanding of ourselves. The first chapter will examine Hocking's alternative style of thought, the "broadened empiricism." He thinks that if the scientific method is accepted as the single valid approach to the study of man and society, both liberty and community will be weakened. The reliance on the scientific method tends, as Wolin states, "to support the aggregate and to denigrate the individual."[27] And men are united by bonds of fellow-feeling and mutual commitment, bonds which cannot be grasped by the scientific method alone. It will be argued that the widened empiricism that Hocking formulates must be included in an acceptable approach to the study of man. The first chapter will conclude with a discussion of his fundamental ethical standard, human potentiality, the value he thinks should guide political action.

Contemporary notions of man in society are greatly affected by the dilemma of modern thought. On the one hand, the freedom and unity of the will are abandoned to various impersonal forces. On the other hand, society is thought to be incompatible with individuality; social relations and routinized social conventions are seen as obstacles to freedom. Individuality is thus questioned as man and society are bifurcated. Hocking announced in *Human Nature and Its Remaking* that

[26] *Ibid.*, p. 172.
[27] Wolin, *op. cit.*, p. 385.

he wished to overcome contemporary assumptions by formulating a "valid basis of an individualistic theory of society."[28] It would be a theory of man that emphasized his free and unified nature through an analysis of the basic structure of the will and its development. It would be a theory of society that did not subsume individuality within social relationships and conventions. Hocking's theory is significant because he so clearly perceives and addresses a central problem of modern thought. Rouner writes that the individual, aside from deciding what he wants, must find a way of relating "to others in such a way that one's individuality is fulfilled without sacrificing the individuality of the other in the process."[29] As important as it is, this is but part of the problem. If a theory of man in society is to be a basis for both liberty and community, it must show that the individual's fulfillment actually *requires* relationships with others. Hocking's individualistic theory of society places the individual's development in a social context. It is the subject of the second chapter.

His discussion of the intrinsic connections between human freedom and sociality provides the point of departure for his theory of the political community, the focus of the third chapter. He realizes that modern political institutions are under attack, that increasing numbers of people question whether political participation can be meaningful. He confronts the twentieth century theoretical perspectives that challenge the dominant contemporary form of political organization, the state. Then he rejects the widespread assumptions that power is the essence of politics and that the purpose of the political community should not be discussed, for neither assumption helps in the evaluation of existing states. The purpose of the political community is, he argues, to provide those conditions necessary to individual development. By considering the bonds between citizens in terms of the concept of the "will circuit," he shows how genuine political unity and common action can be compatible with individual liberty. He also insists that the concept of sovereignty is misunderstood when it is associated with the notion that the state is absolute, beyond criticism or moral limitation. As the quality of finality in the state's decisions, sovereignty is required for common political action and the fulfillment of the state's purpose. Just as he formulates an "individualistic theory of society," Hocking also develops an individualistic theory of the political community. In his review of *Man and the State*, John Dewey wrote this of

---

[28] *HNR*, p. xi.
[29] *Within Human Experience, op. cit.*, p. 163.

Hocking s theory: "Ultimate emphasis falls upon individuals.... The state is the indispensable means of their realization of themselves, and as an indispensable means it is also an integral part of their achievement of themselves."[30]

Hocking realizes that an individualistic theory of the political community must maintain this tension: political institutions must be limited by a theory of human rights if liberty is to be preserved; and an acceptable approach to individual rights must encourage the fulfillment of political duty. He develops a theory of rights that provides adequate conceptions of political limits and citizen responsibilities. He accepts liberalism's emphasis on the dignity and worth of the individual, but he rejects the extreme individualism that leads to absolute and unconditional claims to rights. His reformulation of liberalism insists that a healthy individualism and a strong, active political community are not simply compatible – they are inseparable. Although some social scientists now argue that high levels of citizen involvement may threaten political stability and effective leadership, he suggests an approach to political participation that will facilitate leadership and fulfill the traditional assumptions of liberal democracy about the value of participation. The fourth chapter concludes with a discussion of his perspective on free expression, a perspective that relates the rights of the individual to the requirements of community.

The final chapter examines Hocking's application of his general political philosophy to problems of liberty and community in international relations. Particular attention is given to his writings on issues of continuing importance. One such question is whether the standards of personal morality are applicable to the relations between states. Avoiding the more excessive formulations of the "idealist" and "realist" positions, he argues that the values of the Western ethical tradition are relevant to international affairs. But these standards must be applied indirectly, through the concept of national experimentation. In regard to the problem of securing international peace, he rejects both isolationism and a superficial internationalism. In the absence of a viable international law and an international organization that could effectively utilize force, he thinks that a "creative diplomacy" is the only basis for peace. He explains what such a diplomacy would mean in the interaction between the contemporary superpowers.

[30] *The New Republic*, March 16, 1927, p. 114.

CHAPTER I

PERSPECTIVES ON THE STUDY OF MAN

THE APPROACH OF POLITICAL PHILOSOPHY

Hocking's inquiry into the nature of man, society, and political institutions is philosophical. He sees that "political problems, domestic or international, always involve us in psychological and philosophical issues."[1] His approach is that of the classical political philosophers – philosophical reflection on the basis of personal immersion in political life and dialogue with other thinkers engaged in similar reflection. He is thus a political philosopher in the tradition of Plato and Aristotle, Augustine and Aquinas, Hobbes and Locke. Since this approach may seem dated, it must be justified before a detailed treatment of his political thought can begin. This chapter is, however, more than an apology for a particular style of inquiry. It explores Hocking's criticism of the method which now dominates the social sciences, and it discusses his justification for the approach of political philosophy.

This skepticism of contemporary social science toward political philosophy is a direct result of the widespread assumption that the study of society and politics should, as one recent President of the American Political Science Association puts it, be "modeled after the methodological assumptions of the natural sciences."[2] The methods of the natural sciences as applied to the social sciences constitute what is widely known as the "behavioral" approach. According to Polsby, Dentler, and Smith, its practitioners seek "to distinguish, for the purposes of their work, between statements asserting a fact and statements asserting a value or preference." Factual statements are those derivable through the scientific method; they "refer to 'things' or events in the real world which can be observed with the human sensory apparatus,

---

[1] "Problems of World Order in the Light of Recent Philosophical Discussion," p. 1117.
[2] David Easton, "The Current Meaning of 'Behavioralism' in Political Science," in *The Limits of Behavioralism in Political Science*, ed. by James C. Charlesworth (Philadelphia: The American Academy of Political and Social Science, 1962), p. 9.

or extensions thereof, and are accessible to more than one competent observer."[3]

This reliance on the methods of the natural sciences does not mean that contemporary behavioral scientists see no place for theoretical inquiry. Theory is assumed to be essential in the social sciences. But many would agree with a leading philosopher of science, Ernest Nagel, who writes that proper theory in the social sciences would "in its method of articulating its concepts and evaluating its evidence" be "continuous with the theories of the natural sciences."[4] Such theory is generally called "empirical theory" because it seeks to make only "factual statements," that is, statements which can be verified through the scientific method. Empirical theorists act as servants of behavioral science in various ways: they order the findings and hypotheses of empirical research; they develop general theories of political systems and behavior that can be a source of empirically testable hypotheses; and they refine and sharpen the methodology of empirical research. According to proponents of "empirical theory," all other theory is "normative," since it consists of "value statements" or "personal preferences" that cannot be empirically verified. This division of theory into "empirical" and "normative" types is even officially made by the American Political Science Association, which also adds the category of "historical" theory. "Historical" theorists are presumably engaged in the study and transmission of writings in the tradition of political philosophy.

Hocking implicitly rejects the division of political theory into these categories. He was a student of the history of political philosophy, not out of antiquarian interest but because he valued the insight into political reality of past political philosophers. He does not make the distinction between empirical and normative theory because he rejects the notion that values and personal involvements must be excluded from political thought. Nor does he believe that a person's normative view of the good life or of the good society can rest only on rationally indefensible personal preferences. He thus rejects the assumption that the scientific method of the natural sciences constitutes the only appropriate approach to the study of man. He adopts the discipline of classical political philosophy, a tradition that sought political wisdom, not simple service to the methodology of the natural sciences.

[3] Nelson W. Polsby, Robert A. Dentler, and Paul A. Smith, editors, *Politics and Social Life* (Boston: Houghton Mifflin Co., 1963), pp. 12-13.
[4] "Problems of Concept and Theory Formation in the Social Sciences," in *Philosophy of the Social Sciences*, ed. by Maurice Natanson (New York: Random House, Inc., 1963), p. 209.

Its wisdom have been founded, Sheldon Wolin states, on personal resources which have now become "sacrificial victim" to the quest for objectivity in the social sciences. These resources consist of "ideas which an intellectually curious and broadly educated person accumulates and which come to govern his intuitions, feelings, perceptions." They can be "summarized as cultural resources and itemized as metaphysics, faith, historical sensibility, or, more broadly, as tacit knowledge."[5]

Metaphysics, one of the personal resources that Wolin mentions, received Hocking's sustained attention over many years. The general reader may, however, be unfamiliar with his metaphysics. Because it influenced other areas of his thought, a brief summary of his perspective may therefore prove helpful. He believes that a person's metaphysics, his view of reality, is crucial to all his experiences. All people have some conception of the nature of reality, some "whole-idea." The religious, for example, are not distinguished from the irreligious because they have a "whole-idea," whereas the latter do not. The religious simply apply a particular set of predicates to their views of reality.[6] "We endeavor to see," Hocking states, "in each object of attention a case, more or less complete, of what reality means to us."[7] Therefore, although one's "whole-idea" is always unfinished, as is all thinking, one should seek relentlessly the *"single principle"* that gives a unified world view.[8]

Hocking thinks the history of metaphysics can be interpreted as a controversy between those believing that reality has the character of physical objects and those believing it has the character of mind. The former are "naturalists," the latter are "idealists." Naturalism insists that nature is "all there is," and nature is understood as "the sum of things and events in a single space and time, subject to a single system of causal laws."[9] Since reality is viewed as a single deterministic system, there is no cause outside nature, no "first cause;" naturalism

---

[5] "Political Theory as a Vocation," *The American Political Science Review* LXIII (December, 1969), pp. 1073-74.
[6] Hocking writes (*MGHE*, p. 142): "The difference between a religious view of the world and a non-religious view lies chiefly in the quality or *character* which is attributed to the world as a whole. It does not lie in the circumstance that the religious mind has a whole-idea, while the nonreligious mind has none: every man must have his whole-idea, and such as it is, it will determine what value existence may have for him. But the critical difference appears in the judgments about the whole; whether this reality of ours is divine, or infernal, or an indifferent universal gravepit. These differences, we may say, are differences in *predicates*, rather than in the subject. . . ."
[7] *Ibid.*, p. 130.
[8] *TP*, p. 384.
[9] *Ibid.*, p. 25.

does not entertain any question as to the source of the causal system. Moreover, naturalism rejects not only one ultimate purpose or meaning to things, but also any concept of human purpose predicated on freedom of decision.[10]

Idealism, on the other hand, contends that the "apparent self-sufficiency of nature is illusory."[11] Idealism is grounded in the experience, so well expressed by Descartes, that the most certain thing in the world is mind rather than nature, and on the assumption that only mind is purposive in character.[12] Purpose is the attachment of meanings to events and the inclusion of those meanings within the intentions of a mind. The existence of purpose requires that reality be mental in character, since "we cannot derive mentality from anything less than mentality, nor objective fact from anything less than objective fact."[13] Although the causal system of naturalism cannot admit purpose, purpose may include causation, as when a person utilizes causal relationships to achieve an end. Hocking himself believes that "the world as a whole is at once a purposive order and a causal order in its main outlines, with the causal order inside of the purpose, not the fragments of purpose inside the total realm of cause."[14] His metaphysical position, because it grounds purpose in reality itself, undoubtedly influenced his epistemology, for he sought an approach to the study of man that could understand human purpose and freedom without distortion.

THE BROADENED EMPIRICISM: CRITICAL STATEMENT

Hocking once praised his friend Gabriel Marcel for developing an aspect of "the broadened and heightened empiricism which may very well be, in its completion, the major achievement in epistemology of this present century."[15] Hocking could be so appreciative of Marcel's work because he was himself constantly seeking an approach through which we might comprehend the basic structure of human experience. Although he appreciates the contributions of science to the technological conquest of nature and to increased knowledge generally, he does not think that the scientific method of the natural sciences is

[10] *Ibid.*, pp. 24-41.
[11] *Ibid.*, p. 152.
[12] *PP*, Pt. V, p. 462.
[13] *Ibid.*, p. 471.
[14] *Ibid.*, p. 438.
[15] "Marcel and the Ground Issues of Metaphysics," p. 441.

adequate for understanding all aspects of experience. But before discussing his view of the effects of the application of the scientific
method in the social sciences, the nature of that method should be
outlined.

Hocking states that the physical sciences attempt to master nature
intellectually through public knowledge, knowledge that can be
grasped by anyone who duplicates the procedures through which the
knowledge was originally discovered.[16] Modern science agrees that "a
corporate acceptance of scientific results can be anticipated, and even
compelled, because both the ultimate data and the methods of reasoning from them belong to the field of verifiable evidence."[17] He summarizes this method in terms of three principles.[18] The first is that
facts must be observed with the utmost care. The second consists in
"the discerning of *law* in fact, the process of induction," the effort to
achieve a general truth about the behavior of things. Care in generalization is crucial to science. When one says, " 'Boasting brings bad
luck; rapping wood will help you avoid it,' " he is making a generalization, but not a careful one. Careful generalization requires examination of cases different enough to include all likely varieties in the type
of phenomenon observed and examination of the negative as well as
the positive sides of the cases examined. The generalizations then
formulated are matters of hypothesis rather than direct perception;
the hypothesis needs to be verified and confirmed by the scientific
community. The third principle of the scientific method insists that a
certain kind of hypothesis will not be admitted in the process of
generalization. Purposes are not to be considered. For example,
Aristotle's view that all things strive toward some end is ruled out.
"Bodies do not fall because of any desire to go downward, nor do
bodies approach each other because of any affection for one another."[19]
The full development of modern science occurred when the logic of
mathematical reasoning was applied to these three principles.[20] The
laws of nature were conceived to operate with perfect exactitude, and
it was assumed that everything scientific must be measurable. Mathematics was utilized to deal with the exact measurements required for
the inductive process.

The best known general summaries of the scientific method are in

[16] *CWC*, p. 28.
[17] "Science in Its Relation to Value and Religion," p. 151.
[18] *PP*, Pt. I, pp. 49-51.
[19] "Science in Its Relation to Value and Religion," pp. 152-53.
[20] *PP*, Pt. I, p. 26.

essential agreement with Hocking's formulation. They emphasize the following: observation, the measurement and quantification of what is observed, the formulation of inductive generalizations about regularities in the phenomena, and the systematization and further testing of the findings.[21] According to Wolin, the scientific method comprises a "*vita methodica*," which includes "a specified set of skills, a mode of practice, and an informing ethic." It emphasizes "objectivity, detachment, fidelity to fact, and deference to intersubjective verification by a community of practitioners."[22]

This scientific method of the natural sciences has been transferred to the study of man, society, and politics and is, in fact, now the dominant method of the social sciences. Its proponents believe that its superiority as a method lies in its objectivity, its exclusion of the personal responses, or values, of the knower from the process of knowing. Arnold Brecht explains this position in his widely respected work, *Political Theory*. Brecht writes that only through the scientific method can we formulate generalizations, factual in nature, which can be duplicated by other scientists through the same method. Such generalizations may therefore be transferred from one person to another "as knowledge," Value statements, that is, all statements not derived through the scientific method, may be important for an individual in his personal life, but they are not "intersubjectively transmissible *qua* knowledge." Non-scientific statements are thus not cognitive in the manner of statements that can be verified by different people through the scientific method.[23]

Almost all practitioners of the scientific method would agree with Hocking that value judgments surround the activity of the scientist. Science "lives on that prejudice. . . that it is better to know than not to know," and "it also assumes that its own results will be helpful to other men in the pursuit of their ends, into whose value it does not enquire."[24] Social scientists also agree that values enter the investigator's choice of a topic for study. Moreover, as Hyneman writes, they believe that the scientific method can discover what men do in fact value as well as the "compatibilities and incompatibilities among things valued."[25] The crucial commitment of practitioners of the

[21] See, for example, Arnold Brecht, *Political Theory* (Princeton, New Jersey: Princeton University Press, 1959), pp. 28-29, and Easton, *op. cit.*, pp. 7-8.
[22] "Political Theory as a Vocation," *op. cit.*, pp. 1064.
[23] Brecht, *op. cit.*, pp. 279-81.
[24] "Science in Its Relation to Value and Religion," pp. 154-55.
[25] Charles S. Hyneman, *The Study of Politics* (Urbana, Ill.: University of Illinois Press, 1959), p. 183.

method is, however, that values, since they are non-cognitive, cannot enter the *process* of scientific inquiry.

Hocking rejects the position that values, the personal responses of the knower, can or should be separated from the process of studying man and society. He believes that a proper approach, a "broadened empiricism," must be participatory and experiential in nature. In the first place, he does not think that "facts" and "values" can be rigidly separated, even conceptually. He defines a fact as an "existent object of a single act of attention." Our act of attention outlines a fact, which need not correspond to a demarcation in the object itself. Therefore, the outlines of facts are freely variable. They may be "extensive or minute: a war may be a fact, or a falling snowflake."[26] Facts appear as a raw "stuff," a "grist;" they seem "hard," and "impenetrable." A "value" consists in the human response to an act of attention, to fact. "Value is that aspect of the world which appears when there are *wills* about, that is to say, minds with choices to effect and decisions to make." A value is "that character of being or experience which requires to be estimated in terms of its worth."[27] There is no phase of experience in which we encounter pure fact. There is "no fact without value, no value without fact."[28] The relationship is particularly pronounced in historical and social matters, where a fact can never be found "except through the mouth and eye of some person who has an opinion about it."[29]

The application of the scientific method to the study of man has, Hocking states, resulted in three problems, corresponding to the three principles of the scientific method. First, mental states are very difficult to observe. Second, law cannot be discerned in human phenomena, since it is highly questionable that mental processes follow causal laws – an issue discussed in the next chapter. Third, although purpose is at the center of man, it is removed from consideration in the natural sciences. Because of these difficulties, he concludes that the scientific study of man drifts inevitably toward "behaviorism," the position that only the physical behavior of men will be studied. There is the temptation "to disparage consciousness itself in order to furnish the new science with a measurable and verifiable object."[30] Many social scientists now claim, of course, that the scientific method need not be

---

[26] "Fact and Destiny, II," pp. 322-23.
[27] "Science in Its Relation to Value and Religion," pp. 148-49.
[28] *Ibid.*, p. 149.
[29] *Ibid.*, p. 146.
[30] *Ibid.*, p. 159.

confined to the study of human behavior. David Easton, for example, says that "ideas, motives, feelings, attitudes" can all be studied. We must, he writes, reject the rigid behaviorism of John B. Watson, who held that only behavior can be examined.[31] For this reason, Easton and most other contemporary social scientists prefer the term "behavioralism" to "behaviorism." Hocking referred to "behaviorism." But whatever the term, the central point is that even though mental states are studied through the scientific method, it is widely admitted that the behavioral approach stands or falls by its *method of verification.* This method emphasizes, according to Easton, that "generalizations must be testable, in principle, by reference to relevant behavior."[32] Handy and Kurtz argue that the essential element in behavioral science is "the rule that all *hypotheses be experimentally confirmed by reference to publicly observable changes in behavior.*"[33] Hocking's response to this reductionism lays the groundwork for his broadened empiricism and for his positive conception of human freedom. He analyzes the philosophical assumptions of what he calls "behaviorism."

Behaviorism, Hocking writes, assumes for scientific purposes that the mind must be observable and that bodily actions express states of mind.[34] These actions might be externally visible, such as seeing, or they might, in principle, be the movements of molecules in the brain. Behaviorism rests on two principles: "there is a complete and instant expression of every state of mind in the infinitely delicate and plastic patterns of the body," and "this expression *is the mind* for all scientific purposes."[35] Behaviorism thus assumes that man can be wholly understood by investigating him as an object in nature. Mental states such as feeling, moral conflict, and decision are thought to be causally determined, and purposes are ultimately reduced to the status of illusions.[36]

Hocking questions these assumptions by examining the relationship between the mind and the body.[37] He agrees that the two are related, that the body affects the mind and the mind affects the body. Action requires a body, as does communication with others, and a tired body results in sluggish mental activity. The mind "resides in" the body,

[31] Easton, *op. cit.*, pp. 2-3.
[32] *Ibid.*, p. 7.
[33] Rollo Handy and Paul Kurtz, *A Current Appraisal of the Behavioral Sciences* (Great Barrington, Mass.: Behavioral Research Council, 1963), p. 14.
[34] *SBF*, pp. 18-21.
[35] *Ibid.*, pp. 20-21.
[36] "Science and Its Relation to Value and Religion," pp. 159-60.
[37] *PP*, Pt. V, pp. 448-53.

receiving influences from the body and giving impulses to the body. The mind, however, cannot be reduced to physical causation. The scientist can find "no trace of a physical cause running over into a mental effect; nor can he find any place where such an event could occur."[38] It is impossible even to conceive of such interaction, for we cannot imagine how an electrical disturbance in the brain "causes" a sensation. Although oscillation occurs when there is an image on the retina, an oscillation is not a sensation of light or color or shape. We cannot even conceive of how a sensation is "produced." All we can accept is "simultaneity." When a brain disturbance occurs, at that precise moment a sensation also occurs. The ingredients of the mind – "sensations, ideas, feelings, volitions" – are not the ingredients of physical nature.

Hocking is convinced that since mind is a set of meanings, it cannot be reduced to body. The concept which he introduces to relate mind and body is the "self." The self entertains meanings; physical processes have significance for the self only within those meanings it entertains. The essence of human selfhood is purpose: "The self is indeed a system of behavior," "a system of *purposive behavior*."[39] Therefore, behaviorism's understanding of habitual human behavior is misguided. Habits are not mechanical sets of actions formed like the wearing of a rut in a road. They have significance only in terms of the meaning that a person may attach to repeated behavior. For example, the middle-aged man flying kites may be developing the habit of experimenting with aeronautical problems rather than the habit of flying kites.[40]

Hocking thus provides a philosophical basis for his position that the purposive dimensions of man cannot be reduced to the category of causation, that mind cannot be reduced to body. Moreover, a person's behavior cannot be understood when we know its meaning or significance to him. Hocking's substantive argument for freedom and his discussion of the way the individual guides the process of his own development are both treated in the next chapter. The point emphasized now is that if it is taken as the sole valid approach to the study of man the narrow empricism of the scientific method will distort the human and social reality it studies. The search for "purely descriptive, quasi-physical laws for human phenomena" is quite misguided, "for human behavior, individual or social, cannot be brought cleanly under the

[38] *Ibid.*, p. 449.
[39] *SBF*, p. 46.
[40] *Ibid.*, pp. 39-40.

vista of physical or biological law without denaturing its living real-ity."[41] In such "scientific abstraction" "a fraction of the man is presented as the whole man."[42] Hocking's position is concretely illustrated by the eminent social psychologist, Kenneth B. Clark. In *Dark Ghetto*, his celebrated study of life in Harlem, Clark distinguishes "fact" and "truth." Truth depends on the interpretation of fact by people; it "is related to value and, for that reason, more fully human."[43] He gives examples of what he means.

Delinquency and infant mortality rates do tell us that some people get in trouble with society and that others die early in life. But such facts do not relate the truths of the parents' emotions when confronted with the blight of defeat or death nor do they reveal the individual delinquent, his struggle for self esteem, his pretense at indifference or defiance of his fate, his vulner-ability to hurt, his sense of rejection, his fears, his angers, or his sense of aloneness. These are rejected as facts by most social scientists because they are not now quantifiable.[44]

Hocking's position emphasizes not only that the narrow empiricism of the scientific method is inadequate for understanding man, but that it actually is destructive of human liberty. He writes, "The process of 'objectification' normal to the physical sciences, with its ideal of knifing the thing thought about cleanly off from the thinker, and vice-versa, would, if applied to [human] existence, through its very success destroy the life of its subject matter."[45] This narrow empiricism accus-toms us to see ourselves in terms of "our functions in a well-naturized social order;" "we become abstractions, and lend ourselves to 'tech-niques of degradation' which cultivate the mass mind with its capaci-ties for fanaticism and violence."[46]

Not only does exclusive reliance on the scientific method distort our perception of ourselves, but this method cannot bring an adequate understanding of community. What we need, Hocking states, is an empiricism which "assumes from the start that freedom, purpose, passion, metaphysical outlook, hope – all 'subjective stuff' – are the medium in which every social enterprise has to float."[47] He is within the tradition in social science which has emphasized that society

[41] *EE*, p. 240.
[42] *Ibid.*, p. 241.
[43] (New York: Harper and Row, 1965), p. xxiv.
[44] *Ibid.*, p. xxiii.
[45] "Marcel and the Ground Issues of Metaphysics," p. 444.
[46] *Ibid.* p. 446.
[47] *EE*, p. 243.

cannot be understood except as the meanings which individuals share are known. The great sociologist, Max Weber, argued that social action includes "all human behavior when and in so far as the acting individual attaches a subjective meaning to it."[48] Peter Winch says that it would not even "make sense" conceptually to say that a society can be "explained" if the standards or meanings governing behavior in that society are not known.[49] It is Hocking's contention that the scientific method of the natural sciences cannot in itself comprehend these shared meanings.

Hocking therefore seeks an approach to man and society which rests on the personal involvement of the knower in the process of acquiring knowledge. Such a personal and participatory style of inquiry is necessary if individual freedom and the commitments which are the foundation of community are to be understood and taken seriously. What is needed is an empiricism which *"can arise only from immersion in the material, allowing social realities to show their own logic."*[50]

One matter should be clear at this point: Hocking does not deny that the scientific method may be useful in studying some phenomena. But he cannot accept the assumptions of those social scientists who believe that any knowledge of man and society can be attained only through that method. He wishes to defend an alternative type of knowledge.

THE BROADENED EMPIRICISM: CONSTRUCTIVE STATEMENT

In describing a broadened empiricism Hocking must deal with the key assumption held by many proponents of the scientific method, the assumption that personal or valuational dimensions of human experience, dimensions factored out by the scientific method, cannot be cognitive. It will be recalled that the peculiar virtue of the scientific method is, according to its defenders, that it permits "intersubjectively transmissible" knowledge, because the findings of one scientist can be duplicated by other scientists through the common method. Hocking elaborates the conceptual, intuitive, and emotional aspects of cognition, dimensions which, taken together, constitute an approach that involves the whole self in the act of knowing. After all, he reminds us, the basic goal of the social sciences is to make sense of an array of

---

[48] Quoted by Natanson, *op. cit.*, p. 274.
[49] *The Idea of a Social Science* (London: Routledge and Paul, 1958).
[50] *EE.* p. 244.

particulars by deriving "certain generalities which afford light and order among the particular facts or phenomena."[51]

The conceptual aspects of knowledge cannot, Hocking believes, be divorced from its other dimensions. Man thinks with ideas or concepts; all ideas are "of" something. They are equipment for our "attentive adjustment to the world in experience," and experience is always by a self (subject) of a not-self (object). Ideas classify by setting some things off from others, and reasoning is a process of making connections between ideas.[52] But there is a problem with conceptual or intellectual knowledge. It is *external*, involving no intimate awareness of the object; it is *relative* to the particular interest of the knower; and it is *abstract* or *partial* because it apprehends its object from only one of an indefinite number of possible perspectives. "In sum, intellect *analyzes*, and cannot recompose."[53] Yet, in our act of attention we experience objects within a context, a whole. The idea of this whole is present while attention is focused on a given fact within the whole, and the individual is aware that the fact is in a context. In all our experience we relate the part to the whole and the whole to the part. Hocking formalizes this process as the "principle of alternation." It means that our knowledge "grows from a sketch, in which the whole is outlined and parts are placed by internal development of structure and detail. Induction and generalization do not proceed *in vacuo*: the shapes they assume are *elicited* by the preconceived whole."[54]

Hocking shows that because every idea or concept occurs within a more comprehensive context, human knowledge can never be reduced to statements which are empirically verifiable through the scientific method. No statement could factor out the concepts it contains from the contextual awareness giving meaning to every concept. This point is supported by Michael Polanyi, who writes in *Personal Knowledge* that one's "focal awareness" – the awareness of the object or situation on which the attention is focused – is always rooted in a "subsidiary awareness." Polanyi concludes, "We can know more than we can tell and we can tell nothing without relying on an awareness of things we may not be able to tell."[55] How then are the "wholes," the contexts, grasped? Hocking's answer is through "intuition." "*Knowledge begins*

---

[51] *Ibid.*, p. 237.
[52] *MGHE*, p. 88.
[53] *TP*, pp. 120-21.
[54] "Some Second Principles," p. 394.
[55] (New York: Harper and Row, 1964), p. 2.

with intuition: and intuition is always ahead."[56] A person is one example of a whole that cannot be known apart from intuition. "We do not know living things, persons, by beginning (as empiricism suggests) with the parts and building up the whole: we perceive the whole from the beginning. Knowledge grows in detail; and the detail can be placed because the frame of the whole is there to place it."[57] Wisdom thus requires the union of intellect and intuition.

No form of experience is more castigated by practitioners of the scientific method than emotional experience. Hocking thinks, however, that emotion is not necessarily contrary to intellect. The real contrast to feeling "is not thought but callousness."[58] And *"wherever there is feeling, there is cognition."*[59] Feeling pushes us toward further experience and toward action. It is "that inner stirring which is evoked by the qualities or values of objects – their agreeableness or disagreeableness, their auspiciousness or menace, their beauty or ugliness, their grandeur or dullness, their rightness or wrongness."[60] The following are examples of cognitive emotions: fear and anger, because they involve the recognition that the world is unbalanced and calls for action; laughter, because it is a rapid concentration of ideas, as in "seeing the point" of a joke; and sympathy, for it is "objectivity of mind, and objectivity of mind is *knowing*."[61]

This process of personal involvement through which men and society are known is inductive, for it leads to generalizations, or hypotheses. An hypothesis may be formulated as "the result of a *coup d'oeil* on the part of a mind that has immersed itself profoundly in the multitudes of facts. *Intuitive induction*, we may call it. This was the method of Aristotle, and since his great example the favorite method of political theory."[62] Proponents of the scientific method argue, of course, that all hypotheses must be tested through that method. They often speak of the importance of a "null hypothesis," an hypothesis that sets forth the conditions under which the actual hypothesis could be disproven through the scientific method.[63] Hocking argues that hypotheses must of course be tested, but that this can occur through the continuing experience of the total

[56] *TP*, p. 130.
[57] *Ibid.*, p. 131.
[58] *HNR*, p. 105.
[59] *TP*, p. 113.
[60] *PP*, Pt. 1, p. 53.
[61] *TP*, pp. 113-14. This view that the emotions are cognitive is supported by the British philosopher John MacMurray in *Reason and Emotion* (London: Faber and Faber, Ltd., 1962).
[62] *MATS*, p. 108.
[63] Polsby, Dentler, and Smith, *op. cit.*, p. 7.

self. The hypotheses of the broadened empiricism are judged according to "their power, or lack of power, to express simply the facts of experience."[64]

This testing process is "dialectical" in character. " 'Dialectic' is a rather pedantic term for a natural procedure: ride your hypothesis until it shows its fallacy – if it does, then correct it."[65] The term "dialectic" is appropriate, for Hocking claims that hypotheses which run counter to experience are revised rather than cancelled; a synthesis emerges with greater power to explain experience. The inductive dialectic is based, in part, on what Hocking calls a "negative pragmatism." Pragmatism itself insists that truth may be established according to the criterion of what "works" in experience. Since, however, determination of what "works" cannot really provide evidence for what is true, the only acceptable pragmatism is a negative one. "The logical error of pragmatism may be stated as a 'false conversion' of 'All true propositions work' into 'All propositions that work are true.' " Hocking concludes that *negative pragmatism* is of use in detecting the presence of error, though positive pragmatism cannot establish truth."[66]

Even if they were to see some merit in Hocking's discussion of the inductive and dialectical character of personal knowledge, those social scientists who utilize the scientific method would still insist that such personal experience cannot bring knowledge that is "intersubjectively transmissible." They would say that we can gain communicable knowledge only through the scientific method, since only through that method can one person verify the findings of another. Hocking insists, however, that hypotheses formulated and tested by an individual through his total experience can be transmitted, for others can go through the stages necessary to the original inductive insights. But real communication between people, as Hocking sees it, is more than simply a duplication by one person of the process through which another acquired inductive hypotheses. Genuine communication is truly dialectical. That is, the inductive insights of different people confront one another. When each searches for the most comprehensive truth and does not simply defend his own inductions, the understanding of each participant is enhanced. When one person's hypothesis is followed "ruthlessly to its extreme conclusions," its inadequacy is

[64] *HNR*, p. 49.
[65] *SIG*, p. 11.
[66] *TP*, p. 107.

shown and it is supplemented by the insights of another. From this dialectical encounter a new hypothesis develops, one that offers a more comprehensive explanation of the subject. The initial hypotheses of the participants are thus not destroyed; they are incorporated into a more inclusive hypothesis. The true hypothesis is a "dialectical survivor, – not the survivor in a Darwinian struggle, for the competitors, instead of being killed off, are preserved after correction in their subordinate places."[67] This dialectical process constitutes a "search for a premise from which the several partial truths represented by the participants may, in their corrected form, be deduced."[68]

More comprehensive hypotheses are more "true" because they demonstrate a deeper grasp of reality. Hocking believes this dialectical process is grounded in our experience of different levels of reality. He thinks "reality," like "self" or "nature," is a "double barreled" concept; it is a concept with a "double boundary."[69] The dialectical process of thought and experience is not a random groping. Each stage of the process uncovers deeper levels of reality, and each discovery is incorporated into the developing awareness of reality. Basic reality is an object of search because the meaning of things does not lie on the surface of events. In the dialectic of experience truth is always arriving, yet never completely arrives. Each level of reality which is grasped is true insofar as it is intrinsically related to deeper truths, but it is destined to give way to those deeper levels of understanding which correspond to a more profound grasp of reality. Therefore, disagreement between two men about questions of value does not necessarily mean that one must be wrong, or that both must be wrong. Each may simply be expressing his understanding of a different level of reality.

The political significance of Hocking's position is this: there are no irreconcilable conflicts between men; a common life based on mutual acceptance and understanding is always possible. His thought is thus relevant to the discussions of "absolutism" and "relativism" which are so often encountered in political thought. The terms "absolutism" and "relativism" are generally used in relation to the degree of certainty assumed for knowledge. Absolutism, the conviction that one's knowledge is certain, is recognized by Hocking as the great bugbear of pragmatism and instrumentalism. He states that the absolutist thinks he has the final truth and only has to read off axioms for them to be accepted

[67] *Ibid.*, p. 284.
[68] *Ibid.*, p. 285.
[69] "Dewey s Concepts of Experience and Nature," pp. 235-38.

by others. The problem with absolutism is that it is dogmatic and closed to other approaches to truth.[70] The relativist also rejects thought, but he often does so because he thinks his opinion is determined.[71] Relativism is, therefore, actually a form of subjectivism denying that human agreement on truth is possible.

Hocking's idea of the double nature of reality provides an escape from the necessity of choice between absolutism and relativism, neither of which can serve as a basis for political community. In a political sense, the chief problem of absolutism is its tendency to cause intolerance of divergent views. The main problem of relativism is its tendency to undercut the convictions essential to human action.[72] But Hocking believes a person can simultaneously hold these two things present in his mind: he can think his own present grasp of truth is, in a sense, "certain" because it attains that level of truth which is now available; and he can also realize that others have something to offer to a deeper grasp of reality.

Hocking's broadened empiricism emphasizes the participation of the whole self in the act of knowing, an act that has conceptual, intuitive, and emotional dimensions. Inductive hypotheses are formulated and are evaluated dialectically through the continuing experience of the individual. These inductive generalizations are communicated interpersonally and revised through dialogue, a process which leads to a deeper mutual awareness of truth. The cognitive style which Hocking explains and defends is the traditional approach of political philosophy. It is a form of inquiry which supports both liberty and community. Unlike a narrow empiricism, the broadened empiricism does not factor out aspects of experience which cannot be fitted into the scientific method. Forms of experience relegated to a "non-cognitive" limbo by the scientific method return in the broadened empiricism to a place of importance in our understanding of man and society. This broadened empiricism furthers a more vital sense of freedom for the individual, because all aspects of experience are thought significant. Moreover, community is strengthened by the dialectical dimensions of the broadened empiricism. The mutual quest, through dialogue, for deeper levels of understanding is itself an act of sharing in which men are bound more closely to one another. True community, to be discussed in later chapters, requires mutual respect between men who accept the importance of what others can offer to their own understanding.

[70] "Action and Certainty," p. 227.
[71] "The New Way of Thinking," p. 4.
[72] "Action and Certainty," pp. 236-37.

THE BASIC ETHICAL STANDARD: HUMAN POTENTIALITY

The two previous sections have presented Hocking's broadened empiricism as an epistemological alternative to that type of social science which exclusively employs the scientific method. But there has been no specific discussion of Hocking's ethics, his approach to the fundamental standards which ought to govern human affairs. Such a discussion is not thought important by many practitioners of the scientific method and by "empirical theorists." In accepting the fact-value distinction of positivism, they assume there is a "logical gulf" between factual statements and value statements. This means that a value statement can never be deduced from a factual statement, that an "ought" cannot be inferred from an "is." First-order value statements are seen to be "non-cognitive" and thus rationally indefensible, since they cannot be verified through the scientific method.[73] One proponent of this position, Felix Oppenheim, admits that values are unavoidable, but he believes they rest on personal preferences alone. It will be worthwhile to quote Oppenheim at length:

I have not excluded the word "justice" from my vocabulary. I do not claim that the statement: "democracy is good" is meaningless. I do not prohibit social scientists and others from making value judgments. I do maintain that value words, and intrinsic value judgments in which they occur, have expressive and directive, rather than cognitive, meanings. I do deny the possibility of *demonstrating* that democracy is good and tyranny evil. . . . This need not, and does not, prevent me from expressing my approval of democracy and denouncing tyranny. It is one thing to commit oneself to some moral principle; it is another to claim that it is demonstrable.[74]

Because they conceive of value statements as non-cognitive, theorists such as Oppenheim would rule out that normative inquiry of traditional political philosophy into the nature of the good life and the good society. But since human action, including political action, is always founded on some set of values, those who abandon disciplined inquiry into normative questions are really saying that our fundamental choices are irrational. Most people would find such a position unacceptable. An example of its fruits lies in Oppenheim's statement, quoted above, that it is not possible to demonstrate that democracy is good and tyranny evil. If this is where we are led by "value-free" social science, there is good reason to question its relevance to the social and political issues of our day.

[73] Brecht, *op. cit.*, pp. 126-28.
[74] *Moral Principles in Political Philosophy* (New York: Random House, Inc., 1968), p. 179.

Hocking cannot accept the notion that there is no defensible ethical principle to guide our judgment. When we are told there is no principle of " 'ought' but only an 'is,' it is our weariness and not our wisdom that tends to acquiesce."[75] His analysis of selfhood insists, as Chapter Two will show, that the individual formulates standards to guide his choices; the will inheres in that central policy of the self toward choice. Having standards of behavior "is the most specific way in which man keeps reminding himself of what he is not, but can be, as well as what he is. It has something to do with the use of the word 'ought': my standard is what I think I ought to reach."[76] Because the individual accepts his standards with a sense of "oughtness," they take on an ethical character. Therefore, no man can void ethical values. The only question is whether those he adopts will be reasonable and appropriate to his nature.

Hocking explores the fact-value distinction to see whether the "ought" of ethical duty may rest on something other than personal prejudice. He is aware that some persons influenced by natural science have tried to bridge the gulf between the "is" and the "ought" by interpreting the latter in terms of the former.[77] In this view man is thought embedded in nature, from which he is asked to take ethical guidance. Hocking states that when the biologist turns moralist he generally takes a picture of independence, cooperation, and totality as his model. His model is the organism, an assemblage of functions in which "each is a means to all the rest and to the whole as ends." This approach does not establish an adequate ethical position, Hocking writes, for the harmony of functions within an organism is not voluntary. Moreover, society differs from all organisms in the relative autonomy of its units. To say that the moral man, the man with proper standards, is he who promotes relations within society like those in the organism is to say that men ought to accomplish freely what in the organism nature accomplishes unfreely. Such a position only posits ethical conduct as conduct which resolves the antithesis between the individual and society. This is not a solution but simply a statement of the problem.

Hocking should probably also have considered another approach adopted by some social scientists and theorists, including Arnold Brecht.[78] This perspective tries, according to Alfred Cobban, to determine empirically "whether there are any ethical laws which are

[75] "Science in Its Relation to Value and Religion," p. 164.
[76] *PP*, Pt. I, p. 40.
[77] "Science in Its Relation to Value and Religion," pp. 171-82.
[78] Brecht, *op. cit.*, Ch. X.

universally recognized by all mankind, and which can be deduced from human behavior, not as abstract principles of justice, but as actually observed positive conceptions of right."[79] This position, we must conclude, is inadequate because it avoids the question at issue. We cannot assume that some particular value is more true or moral than others simply because we might learn that it is widespread.

Hocking believes it is possible to discover certain ethical principles which are reasonable and in accord with our experience. It is reasonable, for example, that each person should accept this principle: "I ought to value things at their true worth."[80] This principle depends, of course, on what *can* be achieved – the deaf person has no duty to enjoy music. Such a principle, if acknowledged, would require one to accept this corollary: "When the existence of something better in the world depends on efforts which I can make. . ., I 'ought' to make these efforts."[81] The ethical significance of these principles is more apparent when they are applied to human relationships. To value other people at their true worth, Hocking continues, is to treat them "as what they are."[82] Yet, Hocking develops an extensive argument – one analyzed in Chapter Two – that no individual can be completely identified with his state of mind or his skills at any one time. It is entirely in keeping with the concept of the double nature of reality, discussed above, that human nature be "double," and Hocking believes it is fully consistent with our experience to conclude that within every individual there are deeper levels of potentiality. Men are thus not treated in terms of what they are unless they are treated "*as what they may become.*"[83] And since the unfolding of human potentiality is often dependent on what others can do or provide, the most basic ethical principle must be formulated in this way: "*Treat human beings according to what they may become with the best available aid, and our own.*"[84]

There is therefore for Hocking no unbridgeable gulf between fact and value. The "ought" of man's duty rests in the "is" of human potentiality. "In every form," he writes, "the 'ought' must have its rootage in the actual, including those possibilities of the human self which are actual possibilities."[85] He thus shares the emphasis of classical political theory that ethical norms cannot be divorced from

---

[79] *The Crisis of Civilization* (London: Jonathan Cape, Ltd., 1941), p. 105.
[80] "Science in Its Relation to Value and Religion," p. 186.
[81] *Ibid.*, p. 188.
[82] *SWP*, p. 511.
[83] *Ibid.*
[84] *Ibid.*, p. 514.
[85] "Science in Its Relation to Value and Religion," p. 187.

existent reality but are grounded in its deeper potentialities. He cannot agree with those contemporary social scientists who think traditional political philosophy irrelevant because it deals in norms, or ideals, in contrast to the "real" world of human behavior. He thinks we need not choose between a form of political thought that concerns itself only with what ought to be and one that studies only what exists. These alternatives are transcended by a style of political and social inquiry that interprets ideals in terms of potentialities.

Hocking writes that the primary ethical principle, human potentiality, is apprehended through the human "moral sense." This moral sense, "conscience," helps us to recognize that "certain behavior increases our hold on reality while certain other behavior diminishes that hold."[86] The moral sense makes possible a form of *a priori* judgment. When Cain killed Abel, "unless the discovered consequence confirmed an uneasy foreboding of his own, already ethical, it could teach him nothing except that he had made an unfortunate decision."[87] Some people might prefer to think that conscience is a product of social conditioning. An explanation of Hocking's answer to this objection must await consideration of his theory of the human will and its development. Conscience, he argues, is not socially derived; rather, it is socially "awakened" by parents and other authorities.[88]

Hocking's discussion of the obligation to develop human potentiality as the most fundamental ethical value is the background for his analysis of human nature and development; it is central to his theory of the purpose of the state; and it is the criterion by which he evaluates law. All political institutions and policies must, he thinks, be oriented toward the fulfillment of human potentiality. In addition to furthering liberty, this ethical standard would, if widely held in a society, also enhance community. By requiring each individual to help others develop their potentialities, the standard would provide a framework of mutual concern between the members of society. Each person would be conscious that he was part of a community which cared for him. Moreover, people would experience a form of sharing satisfying in itself. Genuine interpersonal relationships require that the integrity of each person be respected, and an orientation toward human potentialities would insure such a style of interaction.

[86] *HNR*, p. 123.
[87] "Action and Certainty," p. 235.
[88] *HNR*, p. 115.

CHAPTER II

THE FREE AND SOCIAL SELF

THE CHALLENGE OF SOCIAL THOUGHT

Popular assumptions and contemporary social thought alike now question the possibility of individual freedom or personal unity. The individual is assumed to be buffeted about and split internally by forces over which he has no control. Even his self conception is interpreted in derivative terms. This contemporary vision also makes genuine social relationships problematical. For social experience is not possible if men relate as automatons. A theory that places the individual's nature and development largely within his own control is, Hocking believes, necessary to an acceptable theory of society. And participation in large and small social groups must be essential to the individual's fulfillment if social relationships are to be more than mere additional restrictions on his liberty. An "individualistic theory of society" must not only defend human freedom and sociality, but also must integrally relate the two. Hocking develops such a theory and argues that it offers a more comprehensive analysis of human experience than other twentieth century alternatives.

There are two basic modern approaches that interpret human thought and behavior in a deterministic fashion. One approach stresses biological determinism, the other social conditioning. The former emphasizes heredity, the latter the social environment. The view that man, like the lower animals, is biologically determined by inherited instincts was popular, according to Lindesmith and Strauss, during the last decades of the nineteenth century and the first two of the twentieth. They go on to say that this approach "is today largely a dead issue in the social sciences."[1] If this were true, Hocking's rejection of this view would not be so important for us today. But Lindesmith and Strauss may have been premature in their obituary on the

[1] Alfred R. Lindesmith and Anselm L. Strauss, *Social Psychology* (New York: Holt, Rinehart and Winston, 1968), p. 10.

instinctual theory. Perhaps because of the persistence of wars and other forms of combative behavior, the writings of Konrad Lorenz and Anthony Storr on human aggression are receiving great attention.[2] There is also renewed discussion about the possibility of specifying other instincts, such as the drive for "territoriality" that Robert Ardrey has examined.[3] Moreover, the closely related psychic determinism of Freudian theory has never been superseded by all schools of psychoanalytic thought, and it continues to influence public thinking. "The deeply rooted belief in psychic freedom and choice," Freud wrote, "is quite unscientific and must give ground before the claims of a determinism which governs mental life."[4]

The other perspective on the study of man is probably now dominant in the social sciences. It sees the development of the personality as a process by which the individual accepts social roles and conforms to the expectations of others. The term generally applied to this learning process, "socialization," is not new. In 1918 Hocking stated, " 'Socialization' is [currently] the last word in human development; and society is always right."[5] During the last two decades there has been accelerating interest in "political socialization." A growing body of literature is accumulating under this label, and its study is often now regarded as a separate subfield of political science.

Kenneth P. Langton defines "political socialization" as "the process, mediated through various agencies of society, by which an individual learns politically relevant attitudinal dispositions and behavior patterns."[6] Another author states that the individual "so makes these norms and behaviors his own – internalizes them – that to him they appear to be right, just, and moral."[7] Most writers in this area would agree with one pioneering author, Herbert H. Hyman, when he refers to political behavior as "*learned*" behavior, a fact that is "patently the case."[8] Fred I. Greenstein, a respected political scientist, argues that "behavior will be a consequence partly of situational stimuli and partly of the person's psychological dispositions. And the latter are learned or 'socialized.' "[9] If the individual is interpreted in

[2] See Konrad Lorenz, *On Aggression* (London: Methuen, 1966), and Anthony Storr, *Human Aggression* (New York: Bantom Books, 1970).
[3] *The Territorial Imperative* (London: Collins, 1967).
[4] *General Introduction to Psychoanalysis*, trans. by Joan Riviera (New York: Garden City Publishing Co., 1938), p. 95.
[5] *HNR*, p. xi.
[6] *Political Socialization* (New York: Oxford University Press, 1969), p. 5.
[7] Roberto S. Sigel, ed., *Learning About Politics* (New York: Random House, 1970), p. xii.
[8] *Political Socialization* (New York: The Free Press, 1959), p. 9.
[9] "A note on the Ambiguity of 'Political Socialization': Definitions, Criticisms, and

this fashion, we may ask what has happened to his freedom, creativity, and personal unity. Orville Brim, Jr., articulates the answer of much socialization theory so well that he should be quoted at length.

> The learned repertoire of roles is the personality. There is nothing else. There is no "core" personality underneath the behavior and feelings; there is no "central" monolithic self which lies beneath its various external manifestations.
> But, one says, what then of the self? The answer is that the "self" is a composite of many selves, each of them consisting of a set of self-perceptions which are specific to one or another major role, specific to the expectations of one or another significant reference group. The self-perceptions are of how one measures up to these expectations with respect to behaving adequately, possessing the right motives, producing the right results.[10]

This point of view is so inimical to man's sense of freedom and personal unity that it would seem to require a most rigorous defense. But most writers on "socialization" never develop a general theory of man. There is one philosopher, however, who does elaborate such a theory. George Herbert Mead is often advanced as one of the most seminal social thinkers of the twentieth century. He is the theorist most important to that school of social psychology known as "symbolic interactionism." M. Brewster Smith reports that his theory is especially crucial to those who conceive the interaction process of role relationships in interpersonal terms.[11] A brief summary of Mead's perspective will help to clarify the problems of socialization theory.[12] Mead also studied in Harvard's great philosophy department, approximately ten years before Hocking. From 1893 until his death in 1931 he taught at the University of Chicago. He published very little during his lifetime; his major works were collected from class lectures and unpublished manuscripts and published after his death. This is probably why Hocking does not mention Mead in his books on human nature and society published during the decade 1918-1928.

Through analysis of the development of mind and selfhood, Mead formulates a theory of the "social individual." All animals respond to

Strategies of Inquiry," *Journal of Politics* XXXII (November, 1970), p. 973.

[10] "Personality Development as Role-Learning," in *Personality Development in Children*, ed. by Ira Iscoe and Harold W. Stevenson (Austin: University of Texas Press, 1960), p. 148.

[11] M. Brewster Smith, "Competence and Socialization," in *Socialization and Society*, ed. by John A. Clausen (Boston: Little, Brown and Co., 1968), p. 276.

[12] This section is indebted to the summaries of Mead's philosophy offered by Gibson Winter in *Elements for a Social Ethic* (New York: The Macmillan Co., 1966), and Paul E. Pfeutze in *Self, Society, Existence* (New York: Harper and Bros., 1961). These authors were especially helpful in pointing out crucial passages in Mead's works.

one another, he states. In the dogfight, for example, the move of one
animal is countered by the move of the other. Yet, this rudimentary
"conversation of gestures" is not communication. Human communication is possible when gestures become "significant symbols," that is,
"when they implicitly arouse in an individual making them the same
responses which they explicitly arouse... in other individuals."[13]
Due to his unique capacity for language, the human being can respond
to his own "vocal gestures" as others are aroused to respond. Mead
then draws a radical conclusion: "We are in possession of selves in so
far as we can and do take the attitudes of others toward ourselves and
respond to those attitudes."[14] The individual "enters his own experience as a self or individual not directly or immediately," but only
"in so far as he first becomes an object to himself. . .; and he becomes
an object to himself only by taking the attitudes of other individuals
toward himself."[15] The individual thus experiences himself only
indirectly, "from the particular standpoints of other individual members of the same social group, or from the generalized standpoint of the
social group to which he belongs."[16] From his total interaction with
other people he derives his concept of the "generalized other."
Pfeutze writes that Mead uses this concept of the "generalized other"
to mean "a kind of corporate individual, a plural noun, a composite
photograph which a self composes of the other members of his society."[17] For Mead, the individual's self-image thus consists in his interpretation of himself through the composite responses of others.

Because he traces individual development to the viewpoints of
others, any concept of individual freedom or a unified will is problematical in Mead's theory. Although he believes in the uniqueness and
potential creativity of the self, he can give no basis for this assumption. In terms of his theory, he can only emphasize the individual's
"particular heredity and position which distinguishes him from any-
body else."[18] He thinks "each individual self within that [social] process, while it reflects in its organized structure the behavior pattern of
that process as a whole, does so from its own particular and unique
standpoint."[19] This is not sound. It is true that each individual may be

[13] *Mind, Self and Society* (Chicago: University of Chicago Press, 1934), p. 47.
[14] *The Philosophy of the Present*, ed. by Arthur E. Murphy (LaSalle, Ill.: The Open Court
Publishing Co., 1959), p. 189.
[15] *Mind, Self and Society*, p. 138.
[16] *Ibid.*
[17] Pfeutz, *op. cit.*, p. 84.
[18] *Mind, Self and Society*, p. 200.
[19] *Ibid.*, p. 201.

molded differently by the social process, because of his particular situation and the set of interactions he has experienced. But to say that society has affected each person in a unique way is not to say that each is unique. Free, creative, integral selfhood is not possible unless the individual can think and act in ways undetermined by his previous social interaction and role participation. Because he loses the uniqueness of the individual, Mead can also offer no foundation for social change. He writes, "We are engaged in a conversation in which what we say is listened to by the community and its response is one which is affected by what we have to say."[20] But how can an individual talk back to a community which so completely structures the form and content of his mind? In Mead's theory anything the individual might say to the community would be derived from the community.

The poet Robert Burns wrote, "O wad some Pow'r the giftie gie us/ To see oursels as others see us!"[21] Mead's theory and the undefended assertions of contemporary writers on "socialization" tell us that there is no other way for us to see ourselves than as others see us. Hocking cannot accept such a view. If human liberty is to be real the individual must have a unified personality, a personal center through which he freely directs his life. It is to Hocking's theory of the self that we now turn.

FREEDOM, PERSONAL UNITY, AND THE WILL

His analysis of the will and the integral nature of its development is grounded in his non-deterministic conception of human thought and behavior. He believes freedom to be a "primary datum," a fundamental experience. He therefore can only point to this experience and show it is reasonable to accept its reality. A causal explanation of freedom would be absurd, since there can be no "mechanical explanation of the free act."[22] Freedom, he argues, is rooted in the self-transcending quality of the self, the characteristic of human consciousness that was later to receive the attention of Reinhold Niebuhr.[23] The self has "excursive" (observed) and "reflective" (observing) aspects. The "excursive self" is the self entangled in the affairs of the world. It constitutes the subject matter observed by the "reflective self." There is a

---

[20] *Ibid.*, p. 168.
[21] From "To a Louse."
[22] *SBF*, pp. 157-58.
[23] See, for example, Reinhold Niebuhr, *Moral Man and Immoral Society* (New York: Charles Scribner's Sons, 1932), and *The Nature and Destiny of Man* (New York: Charles Scribner's Sons, 1941), pp. 178-240.

degree of independence between the observing self and the observed self. For example, when the self judges itself to be defective or limited in some way, it is "in that act somewhat beyond this defect and limitation: to be somewhat beyond it is a condition of being able to observe it."[24] The reflective self directs the realization of the self's potentialities, a process that would be impossible without free decision.[25]

The self is not completely limited by space and time. It can conceive of more than one space and time realm. With regard to space, Hocking asks how far the top of the tree in the picture we view is from the floor on which we stand, and he asks how far the bear of the dream is from the bedpost of the bed in which we sleep. The questions are meaningless, he answers. These things are simply "not in the same world." From the standpoint of the mind "there are many possible space-worlds, each of which is complete, no one of which interfers in the least with any other."[26] In a like manner, the self is not limited to one time realm. Hocking discusses the self's awareness of plural space and time realms in terms of the concept of the "field." A field relates facts: "*Wherever there are plural Facts of the same kind, there is a Field including them and essential to their being.*"[27] A pluralism of fields is possible, since the mind can conceive of various space-time orders. Moreover, it is only through the self that there can be a relationship between fields. The self is a "vinculum between one field and the other;" it "*functions as a Field of Fields.*"[28]

As a "field of fields" the self can create what the world would not contain apart from its decision. Creativity is possible through "field-replacement" by the self. "The acting self is thus a *continual weaving of other worlds*, self-begotten in thought, *into the texture of the present and given world.*" It "*alters the particulars* of the even sequence of the actual time-space manifold."[29] Each individual must constantly ask himself what kind of world he chooses to live in. We have, at every moment, "the choice before us which of several closely-related future space-time-worlds shall become the continuous prolongation of the past-and-present space-time-world."[30] Of course, man does not always have complete freedom to transfer dream into fact. There is a "greater

[24] *SBF*, p. 151.
[25] *MIHE*, pp. 51-52.
[26] *SBF*, p. 31.
[27] "Fact, Field and Destiny," p. 533.
[28] *Ibid.*, p. 542.
[29] *MIHE*, pp. 229-30.
[30] *SBF*, p. 166.

creativity" and a "lesser creativity."[31] The "greater creativity" consists in conceptual or artistic creations which are completely new to the world. For example, Bach's music was "something which God himself had never thought."[32] The "lesser creativity" is a "novelty of rearrangement rather than a production *ex nihilo*."[33]

Hocking recognizes that freedom cannot be meaningful without personal unity. There must be a central self to direct decisions. He develops his position largely in response to the instinctual interpretation of man. Instinct would be indicated, he writes, by the trend of an entire species toward a distinctive mode of behavior, by untaught skill in pursuing these characteristic ways, and by appropriate corresponding organs.[34] He agrees that man may share with higher forms of animal life instincts such as nutrition (food-getting), reproduction (sexual satisfaction), parental impulse (care of offspring), fear (self-preservation), and curiosity.[35] But there are problems with the instinctual view. He lists three initial difficulties.[36] First, any human instincts are balanced. It is impossible to attribute one instinct to man without, at the same time, attributing an opposing instinct. For example, an instinct of "self-assertion" is no more applicable than an instinct of "self-abasement." Second, there is a variety of pattern in human instincts. There is no simple physiological pattern of sense-stimulus, central adjustment, and muscular response. Different or opposing human instincts use the same physical apparatus. Third, there is a coalescence of instincts; some instinctual satisfactions may vicariously requite others.

The most serious problem with the instinctual interpretation is, however, its inadequate conception of the human mind. Imagine, Hocking writes, a mind that from birth operated only by instinctual impulses.[37] The satisfaction of one impulse would enter the memory. This memory would lend a "tinge of expectation" to the next anticipated instinctual satisfaction, but a later impulse would actually satisfy only as the expectation is fulfilled. The two experiences must be understood as "two *interests*, i.e., as two cases of a common value-meaning." And if there is a common value-meaning, there must be a self which judges whether experiences satisfy. "*Wherever there is a self,*

---

[31] "Fact, Field and Destiny," pp. 544-45.
[32] *MIHE*, p. 63.
[33] "Fact, Field and Destiny," p. 543.
[34] *HNR*, p. 62.
[35] *PP*, Pt. I, pp. 7-8.
[36] *HNR*, pp. 65-67.
[37] *Ibid.*, pp. 89-90.

there all experiences are referred to a common interest."[38] In other words, it is impossible to conceive of an experience satisfying a human mind unless you assume a self with a "common interest" to which experiences are referred. Although men normally experience some inner division of motive and desire, they proceed "on the assumption of a *discoverable unity* of all values. . . and a discoverable unity is, of course, an actual unity, though partly subconscious."[39]

Hocking thinks it is possible to give a more precise account of the development of the free, unified self. The central concept in his theory is the "will." Kenneth A. Megill tells us this concept is now out of favor: "The will has proved to be notoriously difficult to locate, and almost all contemporary philosophers and scientists would reject a theory requiring man to have a will which he can express in a direct, rational manner."[40] Hocking does not believe this concept can be abandoned if we are to have a meaningful conception of the individual. Each person is constantly engaged in the process of acquiring "a more or less stable *policy* toward incoming suggestions and impulses. And to have a stable policy is to have in the specific sense of the word, a *will.*"[41] The will is the self's "acquired interpretation of its own good." It is a rather stable basis for choice. Yet, it changes as the individual comes to understand which choices realize his potentialities and which potentialities are more satisfying when realized. The will thus develops dialectically. One sees that a choice is followed by "an ill-defined sense that one is not, after all, satisfied with *that apparent satisfaction.*" He then reformulates his choice. Or, he may have a favorable "after-image" of the experience and decide to pursue it further.[42] Moreover, because the will is constantly developing, man is a future-oriented

---

[38] *Ibid.*, p. 90. Hocking also shows that man is not simply passive before instinctual forces by pointing out that the "sex drive" may be denied altogether, and other impulses, such as the desire for food, may be drastically affected by conscious decision. See *MATS*, pp. 216-17.

[39] *HNR*, p. 475. Just as he rejects biological determinism, Hocking also attacks the psychic determinism of Freudian theory. He writes that although Freud and his followers have accurately described the original sources of many mental states, they are mistaken in thinking the impulses of the subconscious are other than the self. The subconscious is "that remainder of consciousness which persists outside the sphere to which in our various practical efforts we deliberately narrow our interests." It may be divided into the "allied" subconscious and the "critical" subconscious. The "allied" subconscious is constantly being thought *with* but not *of*; it contains the habits we form – "in short, our 'character.' " The "critical" subconscious consists in matters we have chosen not to be conscious of, but which are still part of the self and may again become conscious through relaxation or reflection. See *MGHE*, pp. 527-28.

[40] *The New Democratic Theory* (New York: The Free Press, 1970), p. 26.

[41] *HNR*, p. 92.

[42] *HNR*, pp. 184-187, and "The Holt-Freudian Ethics and the Ethics of Royce," pp. 495-96.

creature. "My self is my hope; and my hope is forever unfulfilled, and forever reasserted."[43] This conception of the self helps Hocking to avoid the despair of so much contemporary thought. If selfhood is identified with the process by which one decides what actions and experiences are fulfilling, then the future becomes central to the present. Perhaps, it may be interjected, much contemporary despair is rooted not simply in what the individual sees occurring around him – the threat of war and the rapid pace of change – but rather in his inadequate conception of himself.

The development of the will, Hocking continues, is accompanied by an increasing sense of potency. Although we cannot consciously remember how to do the thousands of things that become second nature, the experience of satisfaction from exercising our habits and skills mingles with our new activities, giving us a sense of readiness and power. We experience a general sense of potentiality, an "apperceptive mass" through which we encounter every new task or situation.[44] The desire of the self to maintain and increase its sense of potency constitutes its "will to power."[45] It is the motivation behind even simple everyday attitudes and activities: fear consists in the desire to move from a situation of powerlessness to a situation where one's powers count; in sexuality one discovers the power to bring forth and care for other people; eating is an exercise of power in "surrounding what is alien and making it a part of ourselves": and play develops the sense of mastery in controlled or plastic situations.[46]

Hocking's discussion of the individual in terms of his increasing sense of potentiality is supported by recent writing in social science. M. Brewster Smith reviews extensively the large body of literature that utilizes "competence" as an orienting concept for human development. The concept is proving attractive because it is rooted "in a view of the organism-person as an *active* (rather than merely *reactive*) participant in *interaction* with the environment."[47] Some of the research Smith reviews shows how even lower mammals resist imposed change in their environmental conditions and exhibit a predisposition to determine these conditions for themselves. Rollo May, the respected

[43] *SBF*, p. 116.
[44] *MIHE*, pp. 49-50.
[45] The term, "will to power," is supplemented in some of his later writing with the phrase, "will to reality." See 'On the Present Position of the Theory of Natural Right," p. 558. Also, he refers to the "will to *Shared* Reality" in his last publication, "History and the Absolute," p. 462.
[46] *HNR*, pp. 94-96; *MATS*, p. 310.
[47] Smith, *op. cit.*, p. 274.

psychoanalytic theorist, substantiates from his clinical practice Hocking's conception of the will. May writes that twentieth century man is undergoing a "crisis of will"; even the experience of having a will is doubted. He defines the will as *"the capacity to organize one's self* so that movement in a certain direction or toward a certain goal may take place."[48] Human intentionality is impossible without a will, for every meaning entertained by the self *"has within it a commitment."* Thus, the self cannot know or think without at the same time taking a stance toward the object of its mental focus. It will be helpful to quote May at length.

It is in intentionality and will that the human being experiences his identity. "I" is the "I" of "I can." Descartes was wrong in his famous sentence, "I think, therefore, I am," for identity does not come out of thinking as such.... We could rephrase it, "potentiality is experienced as *mine* – my power, my question – and, therefore, whether it goes over into actuality depends to some extent on me – where I throw my weight, how much I hesitate," and so on. What happens in human experience is "I conceive – I can – I will – I am."[49]

It may be concluded that an adequate conception of the individual would be impossible without a concept of the will similar to that developed by Hocking.

SOCIALITY

The nature of freedom, personal unity, and the will have been discussed in rather individual terms. But if Hocking's philosophy is to be a foundation for community, his theory of the self must have social dimensions. Indeed, sociality must be integrally related to the development of the individual will. It might appear difficult for him to develop a theory of sociality after he attributes to the individual a "will to power." That term has competitive connotations. He therefore prefaces his discussion of sociality with comments on this problem. He realizes that the concept has a savage history, largely because of its association with Frederich Nietzsche.[50] Unlike Nietzsche, Hocking thinks the will to power is not necessarily competitive. The increasing potency of one person does not imply a limited development of the potentiality of others. One person can have more power without others having less. In the language of contemporary game theory, we might

---

[48] *Love and Will* (New York: W. W. Norton and Co., Inc., 1969), p. 218.
[49] *Ibid.*, p. 243.
[50] *HNR*, p. 97.

say that the will to power does not have a "zero-sum" quality; one person's gain is not necessarily another's loss.

Because of his freedom and the unique development of his will, each person has a perspective that distinguishes him from everyone else.[51] In the development and expression of this unique orientation to the world the individual best expresses his potentialities. We need "to inject our reasons and our moral perceptions into the world's work."[52] The will thus reaches maturity "in the form of the will to power through ideas."[53] The acceptance by others of a person's ideas is the most satisfying expression of his potency. In the economic realm scarcity may require one man's gain to be another's loss. But the expression of a person's unique perspective adds to a common fund. Therefore, "the will to power through ideas implies the love and service of mankind."[54]

Hocking's discussion of sociality rests on his concept of the "universality of private experience." The concept is essential if the tendency of modern man toward solipsism is to be overcome. In his last book he even writes that its formulation is "the basis of my first book (1912) and of all my subsequent work."[55] In *The Meaning of God in Human Experience* he argues from the perspective of his metaphysical idealism that the idea of social experience must precede social experience. Otherwise, the perceptions of bodily actions could not be assumed to indicate the presence of other minds. In his later writings he relies less on this argument than on the celebration of our direct awareness of that "*kernal or nucleus* of experience" in which we are "stirred to take our private experience *as universal.*"[56]

Each one knows that this his own hearth-fire is no unique and solitary local blaze: he knows that it is the way existing is experienced by every experiencer.

How does he know that? It is a part of his existing that he does know it.

I say. . . that the assumption that we do thus know is universal. Conversation assumes it.[57]

Hocking is fond of this comment by Alfred North Whitehead in one of their joint seminars at Harvard: "After all, *here we are*! We don't go

[51] *Ibid.*, pp. 227-31.
[52] *Ibid.*, p. 112.
[53] *MATS*, p. 316.
[54] *Ibid.*, p. 318.
[55] *SMN*, p. 10.
[56] "God and the Modern World," (Mimeographed.)
[57] "Marcel and the Ground Issues of Metaphysics," p. 453.

behind that, we begin with it."[58] This fundamental similarity of human experience makes communication possible.

Hocking believes that sociality is too often identified with "gregariousness" or a "herd instinct" like that exhibited by animals. In this view sociality becomes merely a "crowd-mind" proclivity. This mechanical interpretation loses sight of the judgment and will of the individual, since the mental temper of the crowd emphasizes escapism, the illusion of security, and the assuaging of loneliness.[59] An adequate view must show how sociality contributes to the free, unified development of the individual will. There are, he writes, two basic aspects of human sociality. First, individuals desire to associate with one another because association quickens mental activity, speeding the rate and range of the flow of ideas. In communication each sees from the point of view of the other. His mental range is extended. Moreover, "the mental strand of each is not only doubled, but passes from double to multiple as each mind begins to reflect what the other mirrors of itself."[60] Companionship thus increases the value of shared experience.

The second aspect of sociality is this: the individual requires interaction with others to develop his potentialities.[61] In social interaction he recognizes the differences between his standards and those of others, and his policy towards choice is challenged. In thus testing his standards he becomes more certain of their adequacy or inadequacy. "The various standards of self-judgment gain certainty and vigor only in the give and take of the group; there are no more impressive arguments for changing one's ways than the wholly spontaneous reactions of one's fellows."[62] The attraction of friendship consists largely in the recognized possibility of a mutual rectification of standards.

Some may conclude that Hocking's discussion of social relationships in terms of mutual criticism places too little emphasis on the uncritical acceptance by people of one another. But Hocking does not think that criticism is incompatible with mutual acceptance. He simply argues that acceptance is not sufficient as a cement for human relationships. They are more meaningful when they serve to develop the will of each participant. He does realize that we often converse with a friend simply to maintain an "active consciousness of his presence."[63] And criticism

[58] *Ibid.*, p. 447.
[59] *MATS*, pp. 219-24, 269-77.
[60] *HNR*, p. 226.
[61] *Ibid.*, pp. 232-35.
[62] *Ibid.*, p. 173.
[63] *MIHE,* p. 82.

is also tempered by admiration. One often sees a quality in another person that he is only dimly aware of in himself, and he may commit himself to further develop this quality. Admiration is thus a kind of "prestige power" which one person may have in relation to another, but unlike "physical power" or "bargain power," it exists simply when one person possesses attributes or standards desired by another.[64]

SOCIETY AND THE INDIVIDUAL

Since social relationships are essential to the development of the will, Hocking contends that individual freedom cannot be interpreted as either aloofness or capricious self-assertion. True freedom is "concrete"; it requires participation in institutions of the common life.[65] The individual needs to participate in two types of groups. They are distinguished by their size and their social role. Small groups – the family and other primary groups – constitute the "private order"; larger, more impersonal groups constitute the "public order." The two orders are characterized by different values, and each furthers the development of the individual and society in distinct ways.[66]

Participation in the private order brings the individual "confidence, independence, and originality of mind." In fact, *"the success of any man's service depends on a state of mind which the private order keeps alive."*[67] Moreover, the small group helps in the creation and nurture of new ideas. Most new ideas need the friendlier tolerance of the small group, where mutual support encourages the untried. For example, small groups generate new ethical and political conceptions. "In every small group, character plays directly upon character, the effects of moral causes are quickly gathered, surely noted, digested into conversation and built into the traditions of the group."[68] In general, small groups also cultivate the virtues, important to any society – equality, loyalty, reciprocity, and generosity.[69] Hocking is fond of this statement by Thoreau: " 'All the abuses which are the objects of reform are unconsciously amended in the intercourse of friends.' "[70]

While participation in the private order is characterized by love,

---

[64] *HNR*, p. 221; *MATS*, p. 182.
[65] *TP* pp. 210-13.
[66] *HNR*, pp. 302-16; *MATS*, pp. 241-80.
[67] *HNR*, p. 310.
[68] *MATS*, p. 263.
[69] *PP*, Pt. I, p. 81.
[70] *MATS*, p. 265.

participation in the public order is characterized more by ambition.[71] In the public order the individual fulfills his potentialities as he markets his talents by performing socially important functions. More importantly, participation in large groups helps the individual further develop his ideas and standards. His ideas must win their way in the large group before he can be assured of their worth. A person's friends, for example, may approve his theory or poem, but he remains unsure of its value until it achieves wider acceptance. Also, deficiencies in the personal membership bonds uniting the small group may be remedied by more abstract, impersonal relationships.

The value to the individual of large groups will be further analyzed as the political community is considered. It should be clear, however, that Hocking's emphasis on the more impersonal public order is a departure from some contemporary assumptions. Because of their concern about alienation, many persons have come to believe that only face-to-face, personal relationships are important. But in denigrating participation in the public order, they have difficulty attaching value to large social and political institutions. In fact, a growing number of people no longer speak of society in positive terms. Society seems to them a structuring of established behavior that inhibits the individuality of its members. Hocking defines society as "a large community in which conflicts are so managed that the dominant fact is not conflict but harmony and understanding."[72] This harmony and understanding rest on the routine acceptance of conventions or customs.[73] This is the problem: how can individual freedom, spontaneous interpersonal relationships, and social change co-exist with this routinization? Although Hocking's full answer lies in his concept of the political community, a preliminary response is contained in his theory of human nature.

He concedes that even though every society tends to prefer the more developed member to the less developed, all are repressive to some

---

[71] *Ibid.*, pp. 260-66.

[72] *PP*, Pt. I, p. 79.

[73] The transference of its conventions to the young is one task of early education, Hocking writes. Even "indoctrination" is not too harsh a word to apply. But this "indoctrination" furthers the child's development. "Before a completely free will can be brought into being, it is first necessary to bring into being a will. . . And this can only be done by a process so intimate that in doing it the type is inevitably transmitted." (*HNR*, p. 258.) Of course, he continues, during adolescence the young person begins to throw off the authority of his elders; he appropriates values and does not simply imitate them. At this point his educational experience should help and even encourage him to question what he has been taught. See *HNR*, pp. 253-79, *Varieties of Educational Experience*, "Dutch Higher Education – Comparative Impressions of a Visiting Harvard Professor," and "Can Values Be Taught?"

degree. Each looks first to its own interest, and its institutions and customs inevitably hamper the movement of life directed beyond them. This is necessary for social order. Social conventions may, however, further individual development.[74] Conventions contain a society's "accumulated capital of wisdom in the ways of behavior," including the techniques of the transmitted arts and sciences, techniques that no person could learn for himself. Conventions also prolong the "vestibule of satisfaction," the amount of time and the number of processes men go through before satisfying their desires. This helps the individual to gain self-control and to interpret his environment. Nevertheless, the conventions necessary to harmonize the relations among individuals and groups do not determine the individual's potentialities or his self-conception. He is not a social "product." We depend "on society for *self-measurement*, not for self consciousness, not for the raw material of our ideals, certainly not for selfhood." No judgment by another can replace a person's own judgment without his consent: "One who merely repeats or adopts is so far not a mind."[75] Hocking's theory of the individual, discussed above, shows that it would really not make sense to assume that the human mind is determined by social conventions or the generalized opinions of others.

Hocking is also led to view social change as a constantly occurring process. He realizes that the possibility of reform is often discounted with the cynical epithet, "Human nature never changes." To this he replies, "It is human nature to change itself."[76] Men change as they decide to change. "To change human nature is to change *what it wants*, or wills, and nothing can naturalize within the will such a change but the will itself."[77] As individuals change, so society must change. For a society is not simply a bundle of habits, but rather a set of meanings in the minds of its members. A society's conventions and institutions "have to be *thought* in order to be lived in. And because ideas enter so deeply into its constitution, none of its forms are final; it is vulnerable to new and better ideas; it is continually being disturbed by them."[78] The individual never simply takes from custom an exact replica of what is offered. Therefore, men are not locked irrevocably into the social structures of the past. No status quo is ever inevitable.

Hocking fulfills his intended goal. He successfully formulates an

[74] *HNR*, pp. 202-08.
[75] *MATS*, p. 235.
[76] *HNR*, p. 17.
[77] *Ibid.*, p. 172.
[78] *MATS*, p. 315.

"individualistic theory of society." His theory is individualistic in its rejection of both biological and social determinism, two major twentieth century interpretations of man. He shows that neither determinism can do justice to freedom or to the integral development of the will. The self is a unity rather than a multiplicity, purposive rather than determined. He also shows that no determinism can achieve an adequate conception of sociality, for sociality is not a mere mechanical process. Moreover, individuality and sociality are intrinsically related; to fulfill his potentialities the individual must participate in both the public and private orders of society. Man is thus both truly autonomous and truly social. This "individualistic theory of society" makes conceptual sense and is a more comprehensive explanation of human experience than other alternatives. It is the prelude to Hocking's theory of the political community.

CHAPTER III

THE POLITICAL COMMUNITY

THE STATE AS A PROBLEM

Some who agree that Hocking offers a compelling interpretation of the free and social self may question whether liberty and community can be compatible in contemporary political institutions. Cynicism toward the state, the dominant form of political organization of the modern era, is not only becoming more open among the young, but also underlies the unarticulated malaise of large sectors of Western populations. Books with such titles as *The Eclipse of Citizenship*[1] and *The Crisis of Political Imagination*[2] have described how growing numbers of people feel that political participation does not fulfill their deepest needs. Increasing affluence in the West has contributed to what has been called the "privatization" of life, the conviction that one can find his total meaning in family, hobbies, and friends. The World Wars, the Cold War, and the nuclear terror have led many to see that the state can no longer offer great security to its citizens. In fact, some now say that nuclear technology has made it impossible for any state to "protect" its citizens.[3] Increasing numbers therefore echo the words of Emery Reves, "The modern Bastille is the nation-state, no matter whether the jailers are conservative, liberal or socialist."[4] Coupled with this attitude is the growing realization that the state is neither the only possible form of political organization nor the form that has existed throughout human history. In his summary of the relevant anthropological literature, Lawrence Krader shows, however, that the state tends to develop to bring order in complex societies with diverse groups, classes, and associations as well as large populations.[5]

[1] Robert J. Pranger, *The Eclipse of Citizenship* (New York: Holt, Rinehart and Winston, Inc., 1968).
[2] Tinder, *op. cit.*
[3] John H. Herz, "Rise and Demise of the Territorial State," *World Politics*, IX (1957), pp. 473ff.
[4] *The Anatomy of peace* (New York: Harper and Brothers, 1945), p. 270.
[5] *Formation of the State* (Englewood Cliffs, New Jersey: Prentice-Hall, Inc., 1968), pp. 1-28.

Hocking realizes that the generalized feelings of ordinary people concerning the state[6] are affected by two major theoretical orientations. These two perspectives, it should be added, are probably even more significant today than when he published *Man and the State* in 1926. They are anarchism and pluralism. A recent selection of writings about anarchism has exerpted Chapter Seven of *Man and the State*.[7] In this chapter Hocking presents the case *for* anarchism as strongly as he can. The re-publication of this chapter is thus an indirect tribute to the fairness and clarity with which he discusses positions he cannot totally accept. The dialectical method requires this approach. For he assumes he can learn from any position, that the truth lies in synthesis, not in total rejection of any point of view. He argues as powerfully and accurately as possible the alternative positions on the questions he considers.

Anarchism is receiving renewed attention at the present time, particularly among the young. Hocking thinks that since anarchism pushes its argument against the state to its logical conclusion, it is the "necessary background of all political philosophy."[8] The anarchist argues that society should be made up of "free, naturally interlacing, self-governing private groups."[9] Defenders of anarchism, such as Krimerman and Perry, agree that because anarchism emphasizes voluntary rather than coerced social order, the popular image is false. Anarchism does not advocate chaos.[10] Hoffman writes, "The basic anarchist vision is one of a society where all relationships are those of social and economic equals who act together in voluntary cooperation for mutual benefit."[11] Hocking agrees that anarchists think society can be at the same time both forceless and orderly. "The ultimate animus of anarchism is a deep sense of the crime which an enforced organization in-

Krader concludes that "all societies have some form of government (that is, ways of internally ordering their social affairs), but that not all societies achieve this condition by means of the state form of rulership." In societies without the state, the governmental functions are impermanent; they are called into existence to meet some crisis such as a crime or invasion; and they disappear when the crisis is over. The state, on the other hand, has "well-defined, articulated governmental institutions." See pp. 6, 16.

[6] In his theory of the political community, Hocking generally uses the term "state." He also uses the terms "political community," "political rule," and "political life."

[7] Robert Hoffman, ed., *Anarchism* (New York: Atherton Press, 1970), pp. 115-24. Hocking is also mentioned as a source for the meaning of anarchism by William O. Reichert in "Anarchism, Freedom, and Power," *Anarchy*, X, no. 5 (May, 1970), pp. 129-141.

[8] *MATS*, p. 101.

[9] *Ibid.*, p. 90.

[10] Leonard I. Krimerman and Lewis Perry, eds., *Patterns of Anarchy* (Garden City, New York: Doubleday and Co., Inc., 1966), p. 3.

[11] Hoffman, *op. cit.*, p. 9.

flicts upon life, which is by birthright free, individual, varied."[12]
Anarchists believe that coercive authority not only destroys liberty, but
also deprives even good acts of moral value and thus replaces conscience with conformity. And anarchists reserve special reprobation
for the state, because it possesses a near monopoly of the legitimate
means of force – police and the army – and employs the more ultimate
sanctions; it takes "life, liberty, and property." Hocking also thinks
that coercion should not be the central ingredient of human institutions. But, as will be shown, he believes that force, though employed
by the state, is not the essence of political life. It is possible for political
institutions to rest on the commitments of their member individuals.

The other theoretical challenge to the modern state is pluralism.
Unlike anarchism, pluralism does not reject the state altogether. It
focuses instead on the group structure of society. There is a difference
in the way pluralism is understood in Europe and in the United States.
American pluralism, as Darryl Baskin points out, emphasizes an in-
strumental form of associational life in which groups are voluntarily
joined by individuals for the pursuit of their private interests. Baskin
writes, "American pluralism is a chaotic and kaleidoscopic array of
special interest aggregates feverishly seeking to penetrate the policy-
making arena."[13] Because of a feudal past, European pluralism stresses
more personal and concrete membership bonds. Groups are conceived
as traditional rather than artifically created, natural rather than
voluntarily joined. In general, however, both forms of pluralism
assume that membership in social groups is more valuable to the individual than membership in the political community.

Though pluralists generally have little respect for the state, their
reasons may differ. Baskin captures one approach when he describes
pluralism's attempt "to explain the formulation of public policy and
maintenance of public order in terms of the interplay among the
contending group forces in society."[14] These pluralists emphasize,
according to Hocking, that governments are "consciously or unconsciously the creatures of powers greater though less ostensible, – social
powers, and especially economic powers."[15] Theodore Lowi adds that
pluralism tends to break down the "very ethic of government" by
portraying it as "nothing more than another set of mere interest

[12] *MATS*, p. 99.
[13] "American Pluralism: Theory, Practice, and Ideology," *Journal of Politics*, XXXII
(February, 1970), p. 85.
[14] *Ibid.*, p. 73.
[15] *MATS*, p. 84.

groups."[16] An example of the other type of pluralist attack is contained in the work of the American sociologist, Robert A. Nisbet. He argues that the problem with the modern state is "its successive penetrations of man's economic, religious, kinship, and local allegiances, and its revolutionary dislocations of established centers of function and authority."[17] In assuming the functions previously performed by social groups, such as the provision for economic security, the state has, he writes, deprived those groups of real significance to their members.

THE ORIGIN OF THE POLITICAL COMMUNITY

In light of the theoretical challenges of anarchism and pluralism, Hocking concludes that a philosophical examination of the nature and purpose of the political community is necessary. Before he considers its purpose, he analyzes its origin. The genesis of political institutions provides insight into their telos. Although the individual must participate in large and small groups to develop his potentialities, Hocking does not think the political community is a natural outgrowth of human sociality. Large and small groups co-exist in a condition of conflict, and the resolution of the conflict depends on something other than simple sociality.[18] There are, Hocking writes, two basic factors in the relationship between groups and their members that govern group size. First, sociality is, in one sense, quantitative: "The force of the social bond *increases with the number of associates*."[19] The need men have to be with one another tends to unite them into larger and larger groups. Groups tend to expand, because new members are always of some value to present members, even though each additional person makes less difference to present members than those added earlier.

The second factor of group size is the "level of presupposition" that its members can assume. This factor is the reverse of the quantitative factor. The level of presupposition consists in the group's "conductivity," the ease with which a member's ideas can permeate the group. Men are generally drawn to groups in which there will be a high level of presupposition. The level is obviously highest in the group of two. It is threatened by the addition of new members, for they must be "assimilated" through a process that suspends the momentum of the group. A group thus forms "boundaries" when the addition of new

[16] *The End of Liberalism* (New York: W. W. Norton and Co., Inc., 1969), p. 48.
[17] Nisbet, *op. cit.*, p. xx.
[18] *MATS*, pp. 241-56.
[19] *Ibid.*, p. 242.

members would diminish its level of presupposition to an extent out-weighing the advantages brought by new members.

In terms of the value of a group to its members, its extent and its level of presupposition are generally inverse. Thus, large and small groups are at odds.[20] On the one hand, small groups threaten larger groups: the church fears its orders, and the family has often been a hindrance to the development of loyalty to the larger society. Because of its higher level of presupposition, greater loyalty accrues to the small group. Its standards are more relaxed, since there is less neces-sity for the formal conventions which in the large group serve as a "surrogate for understanding." On the other hand, large groups threaten to swallow up small groups by diluting their membership ties. Therefore, simple sociality can result only in a "headless" society characterized by conflict between large and small groups.

Hocking next considers whether economic activity can result in the political organization of society. He acknowledges that economic needs do bring men together for the conquest of nature. But the most characteristic feature of the economy of a "developed society" is a rivalry between competing economic groups. The demand for material goods is a divisive force.[21] The consideration of others only insofar as they are useful to oneself, the essence of the economic motive, militates against social unity. Sociality and economic activity can therefore lead only to conflict within society. This conflict, Hocking argues, can be resolved only through political action. But politics has become a dirty word to millions of citizens. Perhaps their suspicions have been furthered by the conception of politics underlying much scholarship. Politics is defined in some textbooks as "the pursuit for or exercise of power." Lasswell and Kaplan, two widely respected social theorists, write, "A *political act* is one performed in power perspectives."[22] Hocking cannot agree with this view of politics.

He thinks politics includes a "term-making process" and a "com-motive process." First, the "term-making process."[23] It is based on reason, the only foundation for the resolution of conflict. Reason makes possible the construction of mutually acceptable terms of associ-ation, a self-conscious foundation for society. In the term-making pro-cess "association by impulse becomes by degrees association on stated

[20] *Ibid.*, pp. 146-53.
[21] *Ibid.*, p. 289.
[22] Harold D. Lasswell and Abraham Kaplan, *Power and Society* (New Haven: Yale University Press, 1950), p. 240.
[23] *MATS*, pp. 10-21.

grounds and on stated terms."[24] It requires "respect for the differences among men."[25] This term-making activity is the peculiar concern of the politician, the man who "faces both the certainty that men must live together, and the endless uncertainty on what terms they can live together, and who takes upon himself the task of proposing the terms."[26]

Term-making is but part of the political process. The other aspect, the "commotive process," is a "group-forming process" that entails "the moving together of dispersed individuals with dispersed trends of action."[27] It is also a "history-making" process because it involves the union of people who intend over a period of time to act in response to common problems. This passage of individuals from dispersion of intention to unity of purpose does not occur once and for all. All societies are ordinarily in a process of perpetual generation. The commotive process is actually prior to the term-making process. It contains the element of leadership provided by the "statesman," the leader who helps people to recognize common problems and to unite behind common solutions and purposes. While the term-making aspect of politics involves the proposal of terms that will resolve conflict, the commotive aspect consists in the rallying of the members to common action. Although they are distinguishable for purposes of analysis, these two processes are closely related. Each requires and includes the other.

The good leader [statesman] must have in him something of the reflective sense of the arbitrator [politician], anticipating conflicts and settling them, as it were, in advance. Indeed, in many groups, the promoter and the adjuster are the same person.... Likewise a politician, if he is to renew the energies of group-life, must somehow renew the impulse which brought that group into being. He must incorporate something of the promoter in himself;. . . a settlement is not a good settlement if it merely restores harmony or equilibrium among the contestants, without renewing action in a common cause.[28]

The two aspects of politics result in an accumulating set of conflict settlements and commitments to common purposes that are accepted by the members of society. These settlements and commitments develop incrementally over time: "Unless understandings once reached were good for more than one occasion, the political achievement of one day

[24] *Ibid.*, p. 12.
[25] *SWP*, p. 19
[26] *MATS*, p. 13.
[27] *Ibid.*, p. 15.
[28] *Ibid.*, p. 19.

would have to be repeated *in toto* on the next day."[29] Governmental institutions are established to embody past commitments and settlements
and to facilitate them in the future.[30] The political activities of men
thus lead to the development of the political community, in modern
times to the state form of political organization. "The state is a relatively stable artificial social environment, subject to slow change as the
political art adds to its cumulative store of generalizations, legal concepts, principles of settlement, and so perfects its own work."[31] The
state is "artificial" in the sense that it is created by men and serves
human goals. But it is "natural" as well, for "*it is the nature of man to
become artificial.*"[32] It is his nature to assume self-conscious control over
his social destiny, and the state is created to this end. Hocking then
asks whether the substantive purpose of the state can be more precisely specified.

THE PURPOSE OF THE POLITICAL COMMUNITY

Almost all of the great writers in the tradition of political theory agreed
that it was important to discuss the purpose of the political community.
The question of purpose has, however, either been ruled out or ignored
by most contemporary social scientists. The eminent French political
thinker, Bertrand de Jouvenel, writes, "Political theorists, who for so
long devoted themselves to the question of what was right for the
public authority to do, are now concerned only to consider what is the
right manner of its formation."[33] They assume that the issue of purpose
is a value question which cannot be approached through the scientific
method. Just as politics is defined in power terms, the question of
purpose is also reduced to one of power. The political community is
defined as the united power of the community, power organized so as
to be available for many possible purposes. Hocking realizes that this
abandonment of the issue of purpose does free us from "straightjacket
theories of the state purpose" that have sometimes been offered. But

[29] *Ibid.*, p. 23.
[30] In discussing modern governmental institutions Hocking writes quite like a contemporary political scientist. He argues that the termmaking process is most present in legislative
and judicial institutions and executive institutions are especially commotive. He goes on to
say that each set of institutions contains elements of the processes most central to the others.
Moreover, by discussing judicial institutions in terms of these two processes he highlights
their political character. See *Ibid.*, pp. 18-20.
[31] *Ibid.*, p. 33.
[32] *Ibid.*, p. 148.
[33] *Sovereignty: An Inquiry Into the Political Good* (Chicago: University Chicago Press, 1957),
p. xii.

he thinks men will necessarily wish to know whether power is being used legitimately or illegitimately. Since man is purposive, no institution can be understood or justified until its purposes are known. Moreover, he believes that no conception of the possibility or desirable direction of political change is possible if the issue of purpose is avoided.[34] Surely Hocking is correct. Especially in these days of great political ferment, the purpose of the political community cannot be ignored. Unless a viable conception of its purpose can be articulated, the increasing disillusionment with political institutions, and consequently with the possibility of ordered human existence, is likely to increase.

Hocking realizes that to develop his will to power the individual must learn what his powers are, welcome criticism, submit to the process of trial and error, and avoid pretence.[35] Nevertheless, he cannot himself provide the conditions necessary for the fulfillment of his potentialities. This is the purpose of the state. "Briefly, the state exists *to establish the objective conditions for the will to power* in human history."[36] The word "objective" refers to conditions "beyond the control of individuals."[37] The state provides such conditions in three ways: first, it provides "*adequate knowledge and self-judgment;*" second, it ensures the condition of "*permanence*" for the will to power; and third, it fosters "*justice as a state of mind.*"

Individual knowledge and self-judgment is increased by the state as it "*sets the mind free,* by promoting a growing sensitiveness and intelligence in ordering its social connections."[38] Through law men rise above their group life to give it "conscious order and direction." They thus become more rational. Their minds develop as they take conscious direction of their social life. Human reflexiveness, so essential to individual freedom, is furthered. Individuals also gain greater knowledge of the effects of their actions. Every act has consequences on the social context in which everyone must live, consequences which the individual neither comprehends nor intends. Since no one can know the meaning of his acts unless he knows their implications, "it requires the

---

[34] *MATS*, pp. 104-07
[35] *Ibid.*, pp. 321-22.
[36] *Ibid.*, p. 325. Previous to this formulation of the state's purpose, he had suggested a "tentative hypothesis": "*The form of the state's aim is the making of history; its substance is the making of men.*" (*Ibid.*, p. 173). This statement is not inconsistent with his position that the state's purpose is to provide conditions necessary for the achievement of the individual's will to power, a formulation that clarifies and refines the earlier tentative hypothesis. In the tentative hypothesis the term "making history" means that the state acts, and the term "making men" means that it provides conditions for individual fulfillment.
[37] *Ibid.*, p 332.
[38] *Ibid.*, p. 151.

state to tell the individual what his actions mean, and law is the channel of this information."[39]

Knowledge and self-judgment are enhanced in another way. The impersonal law of the state frees the individual from the bonds of traditional groups that he may find constraining. He is freed to join or leave such groups as he chooses, because of his membership in the "perduring sub-community of citizenship."[40] Men become "aware of themselves as ultimate denominators of all social groups."[41] They are able to "keep in place those partial and conflicting standards" of groups in the public and the private orders. The standards of small social groups emphasize fraternity, equality, and kindness; larger economic groups live by prudence, industriousness, enterprise, and efficiency. Political institutions help men to relate and order these differing standards. "In order that valid standards shall be discovered, a community is needed which can survey both the economic and the social groupings of society, gather their long-range workings, and criticize the principles of each in the light of the other, as no individual can do."[42]

By controlling their social destiny through political organization, Hocking thinks men are also provided conditions of relative "permanence." A measure of order and stability are necessary for action, since men do not create unless they expect their creations to endure. They develop potentialities which they think will affect the world that is coming into being. Moreover, the expression of the individual's unique ideas and standards requires not only a "calculable future," but a "cumulative past" as well.[43] Ideas or standards are developed from the dialogue which has as its context the culture of the society, and this culture requires order to flourish.[44] Thus, "the will to power perceives that its way is not secure, in any field, unless the political community is there."[45]

The final way the political community furthers the development of the will to power of individuals is the most controversial. Hocking's argument that it fosters "justice as a state of mind" is likely to strike many as dated, even odd. Two major strands of Western political theory have conditioned us against such a position. Liberal individu-

[39] *Ibid.*, pp. 326-27.
[40] *Ibid.*, p. 119.
[41] *Ibid.*, p. 133.
[42] *Ibid.*, p. 330.
[43] *Ibid.*, p. 119. Hocking acknowledges that the term "calculable future," is taken from Walter Bagehot.
[44] *Ibid.*, p. 118.
[45] *Ibid.*, p. 336.

alists such as John Locke and Thomas Paine, both so influential in America, thought that the state's only purpose is to maintain the minimal order necessary to keep men from threatening the rights of one another. They feared governmental attempts to enforce a state of belief, in part because they had witnessed the conflict caused by governmental attempts to establish particular churches. The price of tolerance, they concluded, was the exclusion of the political order from matters of conscience. In their desire to protect freedom they rigidly separated character and citizenship. It was not thought proper for the state to promote private morals or public virtue.

The other strand of political thought flowed from Kant and found expression in the English idealists, T. H. Green and Bernard Bosanquet. According to Hocking, both accepted Kant's position that law must limit itself to the external or physical behavior of men. Kant argued as follows: "The springs of the inner life simply cannot be enforced; the state cannot promote morality nor religion directly; the attempt to do so can only lend advantage to a hypocritical compliance."[46] In other words, Kant juxtaposes "an anti-anarchistic premiss – that the state must use force – with an anarchistic plea, that force perverts motive."[47] His preoccupation with the nature of the moral will led him, Hocking recognizes, to conclude that the coercion of behavior, which may be necessary, can have no moral quality.

Hocking agrees with Kant that human motivation is essentially inward and free. The political community acts through impersonal law, and "morality moves better from person to person than from an institution to the mass."[48] He realizes that the state "depends for its vitality upon a motivation which it cannot by itself command."[49] He gives more specific examples of what this means. The state alone cannot punish. Effective punishment requires the condemnation of the punisher to be shared by the one punished, and the state cannot insure that the punished will accept the values by which he is condemned. "The degree of goodness that alone can give a penalty the quality of punishment is something the state cannot compel."[50] The state can provide the conditions, equipment, staff, and standards of instruction for educational institutions, but it cannot guarantee that teachers will possess those personal qualities necessary to successful teaching. The

[46] *Ibid.*, pp. 157-58.
[47] *Ibid.*, p. 158n.
[48] *Ibid.*, p. 159.
[49] *CWC*, p. 6.
[50] *Ibid.*, p. 7.

state may provide opportunities for recreation, but it cannot force people to use their idle hours for the self-renewal that comes from genuine art and play rather than for escape and dissipation. The state can establish legal forms for family life, but it cannot "mend by law where the spirit of creative love falters."[51] It cannot insure that prosperity will bring contentment or that labor will be a source of satisfaction. The "good will" can be encouraged by the state, but in the final analysis it cannot be "legally administered."[52] The ultimate springs of proper motivation arise from the soil of art and religion.[53]

Although proper motivation cannot, in the final analysis, be coerced by the state, Hocking argues that the state can indirectly help to develop the moral character of its citizens. He thus rejects the two strands of modern thought discussed above in favor of the tradition in political theory that has stressed the educational role of citizenship. More than any other modern theorist, Rousseau has preserved this tradition. "It is time for us to learn from Rousseau other lessons than those which his own age took from his writings. Laws are not mere regulators of behavior; they are formers of character."[54] Hocking thinks that since the state must direct the actions of its members into nondestructive channels, it must also be concerned about the motives that will lead to acceptable behavior. His position is sound. It would not make sense for the state to define and legislate against crimes without attempting to alter the motives that are likely to lead to criminal behavior. It is indeed unfortunate that today many cry simply for "law and order" and forget to examine the mental states and underlying social conditions that bring violations of the law.

Hocking thinks that law can help evoke more moral attitudes in

---

[51] *Ibid*, p. 10.

[52] *Ibid.*, p. 16.

[53] For Hocking's approach to art and its relation to the political order see *HNR*, pp. 339-50, and "The International Role of Art in Revolutionary Times," Appendix I to *SMN*, pp. 219-230. Hocking's religious philosophy has been extensively examined by others; see especially Rouner, *Within Human Experience, op. cit.*, Pts. I and III and Luther, *op. cit.* Hocking believes that religion is founded in a purposive interpretation of reality which emphasizes that "the world as a whole has an active individual concern for the creatures it has produced." (*HNR*, p. 438). In religion "man apprehends, beyond or within the dark reaches of his environment, a controlling power or powers in some measure akin to himself. If they are not personal, they are at least responsive." (*PP*, Pt. I, p. 33) Religion communicates to the individual "a passion for right living, and for the spread of right living, conceived as a cosmic demand"; it gives rise to the "sense that something in the world I spring from expects me to make a good job of it." ("This is My Faith," pp. 135-36) Religion teaches men that they will be fulfilled only as they are unified with one another. It thus helps them to realize their common dependence and "to keep alive faith in the meeting of minds and the possibility of settlements." (*MATS*, pp. 426-427).

[54] *PLR*, p. 66.

several ways. One way is by establishing standards of justice more general and impersonal than those of less inclusive social groups and institutions.[55] The political community can thus eliminate the "irrelevant disabilities" of individuals. In case some should doubt that the removal of irrelevant disabilities can alter moral attitudes, an example can be cited that would be familiar to many who have first-hand experience with the southern United States. The Civil Rights Movement of the late 1950's and the early 1960's centered in the demand by Negroes and some whites for the removal of laws in the southern states that segregated the races in most tax supported institutions and many private institutions. This movement, often conducted by "direct action" and "non-violent civil disobedience," basically appealed to the Supreme Court, the Congress, and the President of the United States to eliminate segregation laws. Although many racial inequities remain, this movement was highly successful in ending legal segregation. Because the national government forced changes in the racial practices of southern institutions, thus bringing whites and Negroes in closer proximity, the racial prejudices of many whites have been decreased. For example, many white students attest to the change in their racial stereotypes brought about by the integration of the races in public education. It is a slogan among some groups that "you can't legislate morality." Though this slogan is not literally false, its implications are, for legislation can alter the conditions within which changes in moral attitudes can maturate.

The political community can evoke more moral motivation in another way, according to Hocking. Law can create a social environment in which men who wish to be just can act on their principles. A just act in which a person decides against his own interest can have one of two tendencies: it can place the just man at a material disadvantage, so long as his environment is indifferent to his act; it can also change the environment by encouraging similar acts by others. The just man takes a risk in acting, however, because he alone cannot determine which of the two tendencies will prevail. The state is able to make his just act "significant, establishing it as a growing leaven in society, rather than leaving it an isolated deed of heroism or sacrifice."[56] The state can accomplish this, in part, by proscribing behavior that would take advantage of the moral actions of others.

[55] *MATS*, p. 331.
[56] *Ibid.*, p. 161.

THE POLITICAL COMMUNITY AS A WILL CIRCUIT

Hocking's defense of the political community in its contemporary form would be inadequate if it did not include a viable conception of the relationship between individuals and between individuals and the political community. Individuals cannot develop outside a framework of meaningful human relationships. An adequate political theory must therefore show how real bonds can unite the members of the community. Yet, at the same time, such a theory must conceive of these bonds in such a way that the individuality of the members is preserved. The basic theoretical problem is this: can men be politically joined to others without losing their freedom as individuals? There is a corollary: common purposes cannot be shared by the members of the political community unless the bonds between them are sufficiently tight; yet, common purposes will negate individual liberty unless they are freely willed.

In seeking an acceptable view of the bonds between citizens, Hocking analyzes and rejects several conceptions of the political community recurrent in political theory. One view interprets the political community as an organism.[57] This approach argues that the political order is a living thing, composed of functionally related parts. The essential characteristic of an organism, Hocking writes, is that its parts are completely transformed. For example, the soil and air that enter the pumpkin become pumpkin tissue, characteristically pumpkin throughout. In a non-organic conception the parts can be separated and recombined without doing injury to the whole. Hocking realizes that an *"esprit de corps"* is experienced to some degree in all groups, but he cannot accept the analogy of the organism. If the political community functioned like an organism, persons would lose their individuality. The organic analogy conceives of the individual as "embedded as a cell in a body, and at the same time submerged and lost."[58] The organic view could not be accurate, since men, unlike the parts of an organism, can leave many groups to which they belong, including the political community. Moreover, Hocking thinks the unity of the political order must be founded on the free commitments of its members; it is never automatic.

He also cannot accept the conception of the state held by political "idealism." He makes clear that although he is a metaphysical ide-

[57] *Ibid.*, pp. 344-51.
[58] *LEI*, p. 99.

alist, he is not an idealist in political philosophy. Political idealism views the state as an "idea externalized by common consent," an idea representing *"the common reason and conscience of its members."*[59] He realizes that this concept of the state is suggested by a common experience. The individual at times realizes that "the wisest conduct is not what I fully wish.... It is what *I wish I might wish."*[60] A person can be committed to a greater wisdom and to higher moral standards than he can manifest in his life at a given time. Idealism argues that this process of externalization is heightened as the individual associates with others. The externalized standards are thought to be contained in the advice of the fellow citizen. Furthermore, the state is assumed to represent this externalized reason and conscience. The idealist believes that each person recommends to others "that good which he is less than completely inclined to follow for himself."[61] The state is the circuit through which his own moral will returns, but it comes back strengthened by the concurrence of the minds of many others. Idealist theory asserts, "What actually commands in the state. . . is *Judgment,* defined as the best available reason and conscience in the common will."[62] Hocking points out that although idealism has haunted political philosophy through the years, it found its boldest statements in modern times, particularly in the writings of Hegel. Hegel did not think that the ethical idea (reason), the essence of the state, is identical to the conscience and reason of its members. He even spoke as if Reason did not need men to make its way in the world.

Hocking believes that political idealism is "neither sufficient nor entirely accurate." It has three main inadequacies.[63] First, the state cannot embody the entire reason and conscience of its members, since there are many choices, difficult as well as trivial, in which the individual is left to his own judgment. Second, there are other groups than the state that embody reason and conscience. Indeed, all groups help to voice their members' common judgment. Third, actual states "incorporate much that is neither reason nor conscience." There is much unreason, custom, accident, and evil in most.

The idealist perspective has led some theorists to the concept of the "group mind." For example, Royce, Hocking's teacher, had written, "The creator of the English speech is the English people.

[59] *MATS*, p. 44.
[60] *Ibid.*, p. 42.
[61] *Ibid.*, p. 44.
[62] *Ibid.*, p. 45.
[63] *Ibid.*, pp. 49-52.

Hence the English people is itself some sort of mental unit with a mind of its own."[64] To Hocking, the "group mind" expression is only a metaphor that cannot have literal meaning.[65] A mind must have thoughts, purposes, actions, and moral character not identical to those of its members. Such a position is not acceptable because it would imply both that a morally culpable group could contain no innocent individuals and that a group could be punished without harming any of its members. A mind is also capable of pleasure and pain, joy and suffering, and is therefore a necessary object of humane considerations. But some groups may not deserve respect and protection. Finally, because stable groups like states act with varying degrees of intelligence and morality, depending on their particular administration, any personality ascribed would be "strangely hampered in expression by the individual tools it employs."

Hocking cannot accept organicism or political idealism because these positions submerge the individual too completely within the community. Political action based on these conceptions would threaten rather than enhance the development of the individual's will to power. He also rejects any position that would sunder the bonds between men by interpreting individuals as "social atoms." Just as the individual must not be lost to the community, the bonds of community must not be abandoned to an extreme individualism. The concept Hocking believes most appropriate for maintaining both community bonds and individual liberty is the concept of the "vital circuit" or the "will circuit."[66] The self includes "something of its objects."[67] Each individual, Hocking writes, normally acts within a particular routine and region, and he generally utilizes a certain set of tools. The mechanic has his particular bench and tools; the writer has his place of work, his equipment, and his characters; the farmer has his land, tools, stock and routine. "Such extensions of the self of will and habit we may therefore refer to as *vital circuits* in a generalized sense, or specifically as *will circuits*."[68]

Hocking adds that the "common 'third' is, in part, a region of co-

[64] *Ibid.*, pp. 351-52.
[65] *Ibid.*, pp. 351-61.
[66] Hocking was ahead of his time in applying the concept of the "circuit" to the political community. This concept has become important in the political science literature of the 1960's. One of the most important books in political science published during this decade is *The Nerves of Government*, by Karl W. Deutsch (New York: The Free Press, 1966). It utilizes the concept of the "circuit" in an attempt to apply the insights of "cybernetics" to the understanding of political systems.
[67] *MATS*, p. 342.
[68] *Ibid.*, p. 364.

incident selfhood."[69] A kind of union is actually formed as will circuits coincide when individuals share a common purpose and utilize the same physical objects and space. He illustrates this with two drawings:

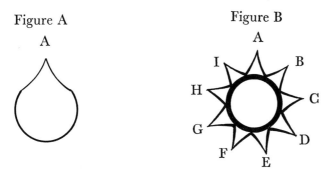

Figure A

A

Figure B

A

I   B

H   C

G   D

F   E

One individual's will circuit (Figure A) is united to the will circuits of other individuals (Figure B). Together they form an autonomous coincident will circuit (dark line in Figure B).[70] The activities of individuals result in the formation of different groups with different coincident circuits.

The coincident circuit of any group appears to the individuals involved to have a degree of autonomy, a "life of its own," especially in larger groups. Each individual comes to look on the coincident circuit "as something which ought to be carried on, which *ought to live*."[71] Hocking thinks it is natural for men to respect the life of groups. "Because one cares for selves one must care for the integrity of whatever forms an integral part of their lives. He who injures a vital circuit injures a self."[72] He thus interprets sociality in terms of the spontaneous and reasonable response of individuals to their group memberships. The human mind has the capacity of becoming "a community of represented minds."[73] Individuals may be genuinely unified within a coincident will circuit without losing their individuality.

The political community is the most comprehensive of coincident will circuits. "*The state is the circuit required by the will to power of each member, coincident for all the people of a defined territory, and including them.*"[74] If citizens interpret the political community as a coincident will cir-

[69] "Marcel and the Ground Issues of Metaphysics," p. 452.
[70] *MATS*, p. 366.
[71] *Ibid.*, p. 367.
[72] *Ibid.*, pp. 367-68.
[73] *Ibid.*, p. 369.
[74] *Ibid.*, p. 371.

cuit, Hocking believes they can experience community and political obligation as well. They will make this commitment: "We cannot drop out of the projects of those past minds into whose circuit we are born; it imposes the expectation of its continuance upon us."[75] Hocking's position does not lose the individual to the political community. Its unity ultimately depends on the extent to which "its circuit is actually used by the will life of its extant members: it lives only so far as it is thought, meant, and reaffirmed by them."[76] For Hocking, political unity must rest on the commitments of individuals to a life of common involvement with one another.

SOVEREIGNTY

The power and coercion exercised by the viable and healthy political community must therefore be grounded in the wills of its individual members.[77] Hocking rejects the argument of those anarchists and "realists" who reduce obedience to law to the state's force or threat of force. He points out that much law really is not enforced. Voluntary obedience is generally strengthened by custom.[78] Although physical coercion must occasionally be employed or threatened, he reminds us that "the constant appeal to force is the sign of a bad disciplinarian."[79] Power alone may secure transitory obedience, but the strong and relatively stable political community rests "essentially on a moral bond." Men are "never governed by fear and force alone, but always in part by conviction and loyalty."[80] The state receives this conviction and loyalty when it embodies and enacts the moral ideals and goals of

[75] *Ibid.*, p. 375.
[76] *Ibid.* Hocking realizes that geographical and historical factors also contribute to the state's unity. He discusses the term "nation," which is often associated with the modern state. A nation is "a psychological fact, a short of composite selfhood." He approves of Vico's definition of a nation as "a community of life and of conscience." Nations may transcend language or race, but a shared place and a shared time – a common geographical habitat and a common history – are fundamental. A common geography imposes the necessity of "common lot." A common history works to erase old hatreds and to elicit a "'we'-consciousness." This "'we'-consciousness" is expressed through a common culture consisting, in part, of shared customs, language, arts, literature, and religion. Although a nation is not necessarily identifiable with a politically organized community, "it is out of a nation that political life most readily springs." See *SWP*, pp. 169-79; *MATS*, p. 267.
[77] Hocking thinks the citizens express their wills in an "act of faith." It resembles the commitment required by Rousseau's *Social Contract*, though it need not be expressed at a specific point in time: "I commit myself and my fortunes without reserve to the reason of this people, surrendering to the organ of our united will command of my physical forces, and assuming that all make the same commitment." See *MATS*, p. 191.
[78] *MATS*, p. 72.
[79] *Ibid.*, p. 192.
[80] "This is My Faith," pp. 26-27.

the people.[81] Hocking concludes, "The physical power of the state is not legitimate unless it is an integral part of its moral power."[82] The commitments of individuals unite this physical and moral power and establish the state's sovereignty.[83]

F. H. Hinsley shows that the concept of "sovereignty" reached full flowering in the writings of early modern theorists such as Bodin, Hobbes, and Grotius.[84] Like most important concepts in the history of political philosophy, it has been the center of much debate.[85] Jacques Maritain argues that the concept should be discarded, since it is "but one with the concept of Absolutism."[86] Some defenders of sovereignty *have* been absolutists. For example, Hobbes assumed that the state could not bring order and security unless it ruled out internal criticism and itself defined all politically relevant moral standards. But Hocking thinks the association of sovereignty with absolutism is a misunderstanding of the concept. Sovereignty does not require the state's exemption from opposition, criticism, or moral limitation. It is rather "the acknowledged right and power of final decision in public acts."[87] It implies, "not the absence of limiting and critical authorities, but the absence of any other power *of the same kind* in a position of superior command."[88] For example, a person may be limited in many ways by his neighbors; there may be things which he " 'wouldn't dare to do.' " Yet, we ordinarily think he is "sovereign," in the sense that his actions emanate from his own judgment.[89]

Hocking's support of free expression and his general view of the relationship between ethical judgment and law are discussed in the following chapter. It should be clear, however, that he desires the moral judgment of the citizen to remain "undazzled and unbought" by the state. He could never have uttered the slogan, "My country, right or wrong." Sovereignty also does not entail a monopoly of authority by the state. He writes that authority springs spontaneously wherever in society men find value in other individuals or groups and wish to emulate or follow them. Aristotle was wrong in his view that

[81] *MATS*, p. 185.

[82] *Ibid.*, p. 192.

[83] *Ibid.*, p. 193.

[84] *Sovereignty* (New York: Basic Books, Inc., 1966).

[85] For pro and con arguments on the usefulness of the concept, see W. J. Stankiewicz, *In Defense of Sovereignty* (New York: Oxford University Press, 1969).

[86] Maritain, *Man and the State* (University of Chicago Press, 1957), pp. 28-53.

[87] *MATS*, p. 194.

[88] *Ibid.*, p. 397.

[89] *Ibid.*

the state embodies the "all inclusive end embracing and superseding the purposes of all personal and family and village life."[90]

Although the state is neither perfect nor beyond moral judgment, it is still *"justified in dictating its experiments*. In abandoning the proposition, This law is absolutely right, it may insist on the proposition, It is absolutely right to try this law."[91] Unless the state can experiment through law, it cannot successfully provide those conditions that will help develop the potentialities of its citizens. If the members of a society are to be able to address and solve their common problems, the state must have a decision-making capacity of "such finality as is necessary to enable the group to carry out common action."[92] To those pluralists who argue that sovereignty only strengthens the power of the groups that control governmental institutions, Hocking replies that without sovereignty there would be no hope of restraining dominant powers in society. The sovereign state can potentially bring order to the relationships between the various groups of society, thus fulfilling the individual's interest in "not being torn asunder by the conflict of his various belongings."[93]

Hocking does recognize, however, that some political orders may fall so far short of these potentialities that the question of revolution is entertained. "The bad government is a familiar fact: the bad state is among the possibilities."[94] A "bad government' serves the interests only of a particular class or group. It is hopeless (a bad state) only when it establishes "a deliberate policy of keeping the exploited masses undeveloped and ignorant" and maintains "a vicious circle out of which the society is unable to move."[95] He realizes that some regimes will refuse to alter such policies. "They will parley, arbitrate, consult their duty, and yield a little; but they do not know how to perform the sacrifice that hurts." They cannot "expand to the measure of the new forces. They must be broken."[96]

Although action against such a state may be justified, the presumption is "always against the violent discontinuity of life. No one who destroys knows all that he destroys. Neither does he know all that he begets."[97] Just as some conservatism is cowardly about needed innova-

---

[90] "Sovereignty and Moral Obligation," p. 315. The quotation is Hocking's.
[91] *MATS*, p. 409.
[92] *Ibid.*, p. 194.
[93] *Ibid.*, p. 398.
[94] *Ibid.*, p. 445.
[95] *Ibid.*, p. 447.
[96] *Ibid.*, p. 448.
[97] *Ibid.*, p. 453.

tions, so some radicalism is perverse in its readiness to leap blindly into unseen evils. Such radicalism may also "set up as the only tangible good the fight itself with its necessary cultivation of unnecessary rancor."[98] Hocking does not believe it is possible to give a specific formula an individual could follow in the momentous decision concerning action against the government. The decision must be made in the "darkness of solitary judgment."[99] But such action should have the character of what Camus calls "rebellion."[100] It should attempt to call the government back to a respect for the common humanity of men.

Just as there is a presumption against revolution, when revolution does occur it will generally reflect real grievances. No measure can be satisfactory if it provokes many "otherwise decent citizens to armed rebellion."[101] The clearest example of a situation in which force, even violence, is appropriate is when a colonial dependency is striving to free itself from external domination. "No people has succeeded in drawing attention to its case of independence unless it has paid a price in suffering, remonstrance, and revolt, even though this may stop short of overt warfare." Moreover, "general interest in the qualifications of such countries for independence has arisen subsequent to their proved capacity to make themselves an intolerable nuisance to their governors."[102] In such circumstances force can also produce the leadership and social cohesion necessary for independent political existence.

By this point some readers may have concluded that Hocking's entire theory pertains too much to some ideal political community, rather than to "real" states. This would be a misunderstanding. He

---

[98] *Ibid.*, p. 452.

[99] *HNR*, p. 282.

[100] Hocking summarizes Camus' position in *The Rebel* (See "God and the Modern World"): "*Revolution*, he [Camus] finds, as violent overturn, exchanges one tyranny for another. *Rebellion* has a different temper. It unites denunciation of the tyrant with *a call for agreement*. It stands up to that tyrant – only, not to destroy him, to *bring him to himself*. He says to him, in effect: 'This which you require of me is *against your own nature* as well as mine: at the peril of my life I refuse to do it, in the name of our common humanity.'
What the Rebel achieves, if he does achieve it, is *solidarity instead of conflict*. He has, by an act of affirmative faith, created a new mind in the tyrant."

[101] *MATS*, p. 393. Hocking supports those "democratic revolutions" which undertake "to render all further revolutions unnecessary by providing within the cover of national order both the method and the disposition for sufficient self-correction." (*MATS*, p. 454). In his last book he states that "*given the democratic republic, no other social revolution is either needful or tolerable*." (*SMN*, p. 122). This position does not, of course, answer the question as to whether any particular government may use democratic forms simply to cover fundamental injustices and to block real change.

[102] "Colonies and Dependent Areas," pp. 24-25. Hocking's statements are the more significant because they were made in 1943, before the Western powers began to free their colonies in Asia and Africa.

concentrates instead on possibilities for the political community which no actual state completely embodies. As a political philosopher, he develops a general theory of the potentialities of the political community. He is correct in believing this task to be important. We cannot learn how to improve existing political institutions unless we have a broad conception of the relationship between the purpose of the political community and the nature of man; we cannot evaluate the ties between citizens or between the citizens and the political order unless we can conceive of these bonds in a way that preserves both liberty and community; and without an adequate concept of sovereignty we can have no theory of effective political action. In summary, just as he formulates an individualistic theory of society, Hocking also develops an individualistic theory of the political community. It is a compelling and original theory, one that maintains individual liberty within a context of community. The following chapter examines his application of this general theory to specific problems that arise when the individual's rights are related to his community responsibilities.

CHAPTER IV

INDIVIDUAL RIGHTS AND COMMUNITY RESPONSIBILITIES

WAYS OF THINKING ABOUT RIGHTS

Hocking's general theory of the political community maintains liberty and community in tension. The purpose of the political order is to develop the potentialities of its members, and the common political action necessary to achieve this purpose and to solve social problems requires the sovereign enforcement of the community's political experiments. The political community must be active and its laws binding; yet, there must be limits on political institutions if liberty is to be preserved. Because of this tension, Hocking cannot avoid the question of human rights. There must be a standard by which individuals can judge whether government acts beyond its proper limits, but it must be a standard that encourages political participation and the performance of political duty, not withdrawal. An adequate conception of rights will protect freedom while maintaining social unity and common political action. Hocking develops such a theory of human rights. It is grounded in his conception of ethical duty and in his theory of human nature and development.

His interest in the nature of rights and their relationship to law was stimulated by his experience in teaching courses with Roscoe Pound, probably the most eminent American legal scholar and lecturer of his generation. They led two seminars together, each lasting for an entire academic year.[1] Hocking recognized his indebtedness to Pound and dedicated *Present Status of the Philosophy of Law and of Rights* to him. In spite of this valuable association, Hocking's legal philosophy is quite original. He maintained his interest in law and rights, publishing important articles exclusively on rights, and in 1947 he delivered Harvard's William James Lectures on the Philosophy of Law.

There are, he writes, four "ways of thinking about rights" that are prevalent in the modern period, each of which is inadequate as it is

[1] The seminars were held in 1920-21 and 1925-26.

now formulated.[2] The first approach is formulated in terms of "natural rights," a concept that has endured in the West since the 17th century. It insists "that all men possess certain rights 'by nature,' irrespective of particular social, legal, or political institutions, and that these can be demonstrated by reason."[3] One of the more famous defenses of this position is John Locke's argument that all men have the natural right to "life, liberty, and property."[4] Another is the reference in the American Declaration of Independence to these "self evident" truths: "that all men are created equal, that they are endowed by their creator with certain unalienable rights, that among these are Life, Liberty, and the pursuit of Happiness."

Hocking finds two problems with the concept of "natural rights." First, people often assume that there are several fundamental rights which "are reasonable in the sense of being self-evident." But there could only be one natural right, since there can be only one absolute standard.[5] There can be "no harmonious plurality of absolutes."[6] The older natural rights philosophy had many absolute rights and conflict between them was inevitable. "With such a nest of absolutes there could be no living. There must be compromise, and as any compromise destroys the claim to absoluteness, the natural outcome of experience was the repudiation of all of them."[7] A second, more serious problem with the concept of natural rights is that it is frequently used to justify the rejection of individual duties. An outmoded, extreme individualism mistakenly conceives of a natural right as "a right with which a person is born, one which he cannot help having, one for which he has paid no price, and has no price to pay, furthermore, one of which he cannot divest himself, and of which no one can deprive him."[8] Hocking thinks such a view will bring social disunity and discourage the performance of community responsibilities.

A second way of thinking about rights interprets them as "historical growths," the "coinage of custom." The greatest exponent of this view was probably Edmund Burke. In reacting to the natural rights position articulated by Thomas Paine in *The Rights of Man*, Burke argued that

[2] See "Ways of Thinking About Rights: A New Theory of the Relation Between Law and Morals."

[3] S. I. Benn and Richard S. Peters, *The Principles of Political Thought* (New York: The Free Press, 1965), p. 109.

[4] See *Second Treatise on Civil Government*, ch. II.

[5] "Ways of Thinking About Rights," p. 246.

[6] "On the Present Position of the Theory of Natural Right," p. 558.

[7] *PLR*, p. 79.

[8] *LEI*, pp. 51-52.

rights are "natural" only in the sense that they develop "naturally" out of historical circumstances. He saw rights in prescriptive terms, as evolving from specific personal and institutional experience.[9] Hocking concludes that the historical approach to rights correctly emphasizes that law is often based on custom. The assumption that rights are limited to custom would, however, mean that reform of custom is always wrong, a position unacceptable to most people.[10] Hocking thinks the historical view is also correct in assuming that man's understanding of rights develops over time. But this approach does not see that ethical judgments about human rights are part of the custom embodied in law. Ethical standards tend to influence law as they become widely shared in the community, as they achieve "the objectivity of an approximately common sense."[11]

The third way of thinking about rights insists that they are derived from the authoritative decision of positive law. This view, often referred to as "positivistic jurisprudence," reached its most famous expression in the work of the English utilitarian, John Austin. The utilitarians wished to abandon the historical and natural rights approaches, because they believed both were obstacles to the reform of English law. Austin argued as follows: law is simply command, the command of a superior to an inferior; and since a legal system must have a determinate superior, laws are ultimately commands of the "sovereign."[12] According to Austin, the science of jurisprudence, "is concerned with positive laws, or with laws strictly so called, as considered without regard to their goodness or badness."[13] This theory of law left no room for considering human rights as other than commands of the sovereign, commands enforced through the legal system. As Benn and Peters point out, Austin ultimately reduces the question of rights to one of power.[14]

Hocking cannot accept the positivist perspective. He argues that a

---

[9] See *Reflections on the Revolution in France*.
[10] "Ways of Thinking About Rights," p. 250.
[11] Hocking summarizes the relationship between law and ethical standards:
"In brief, law falls in behind the advance of ethical reflection, attempting to make unanimous in behavior what ethical sense has made almost unanimous in motive, and in so doing (a) to make the motivation itself more nearly unanimous and (b) to transfer the released ethical energy to a new level of issues, which in turn will eventually become material for new law. Law is the great civilizing agency it is not because it throws conduct into artificial uniformity and order, but because it is a working partner with the advancing ethical sense of the community." See *ibid.*, p. 258.
[12] "Lectures on Jurisprudence," Lectures 5 and 6 in *The Austinian Theory of Law*, ed. by W. Jethro Brown (London: J. Murray, 1906), pp. 96-97.
[13] *Ibid.*, p. 35.
[14] Benn and Peters, *op. cit.*, pp. 103-07.

moral content to human rights is unavoidable. Ethical conceptions are
an intrinsic part of the process by which legal rights are officially
determined, authoritatively enforced, and accepted by the people. In
the first place, the basic nature of the competing interests in a society
is structured by ethical standards. Those things about which conflicts
of interest occur, the goods which people seek, are partially determined
by ethical judgments. "The concrete goods, which are the materials of
adjustment, are themselves subject to ethical estimation."[15] Also, the
law that adjusts these conflicting interests is only effective if it does not
violate the moral standards of the people.[16] Finally, positivists fail to
see that the argument that ethics should not influence law itself rests on
ethical positions.[17] The principle of *stare decisis*, for example, is really
an ethical principle when it is interpreted narrowly to mean that past
legal decisions should always decide future cases. Its central ethical
standard is this: it is morally right to adhere to past decisions, "on the
ground that it is always wrong, other things being equal, to disappoint
an aroused expectation."[18] Such an ethical principle will always be
confronted by other moral standards that demand change in the law.[19]

A fourth approach to rights interprets them as "general conditions
of social welfare."[20] This is the view, for example, of that sociological
jurisprudence that has been so important in the United States. The
orientation of sociological jurisprudence is well-expressed in Roscoe
Pound's statement that law should provide "such an adjustment of relations and ordering of conduct as will make the goods of existence, the
means of satisfying human claims to have things and do things, go
round as far as possible with the least friction and waste."[21] Hocking
also states that rights are perceived as "general conditions of social
welfare" by utilitarianism, by the pragmatism of Duguit and Dewey,
and by the functionalism of Tawney. The common essense of all these

---

[15] "Ways of Thinking About Rights," p. 265.
[16] *Ibid.*, p. 245.
[17] *Ibid.*, p. 258.
[18] *Ibid.*, p. 259.
[19] Hocking thinks another misunderstanding of the relationship between law and ethics in
the work of the legal system is evident in the argument by "legal realists" that courts do not
decide cases on the basis of general principles, but only "make" law in specific cases without
the help of any standards. He concludes that such a position ignores the most general
principle of all, justice. He writes, "Each new case gives us a new chance to perceive what
justice means. In this way, the idea of justice grows." See "Justice, Law, and the Cases,"
p. 333.
[20] "Ways of Thinking About Rights," p. 252.
[21] *Social Control Through Law* (New Haven: Yale University Press, 1942), p. 65. Edward M.
Burns shows that sociological jurisprudence rejected both the historical and natural rights
positions because it thought they neglected actual social needs. See *Ideas in Conflict* (New
York: W. W. Norton and Co., Inc., 1960), pp. 127-134.

schools is the belief that rights "are distributive means to an independently definable social good." This perspective "brings a standard to bear on all existing law which might be called in a broad sense ethical, but it clearly excludes reference to independent ethical rules."[22]

Hocking rejects this general way of thinking because it subordinates individual rights to the social function performed by the individual. It thus provides no vantage point for the criticism of law and policy. Moreover, the approach is circular: if rights are functions of social welfare, then whatever the social welfare requires is right; but if there are to be genuine human rights, they must be determined before the social welfare is considered.[23]

According to Hocking, the failure to solve this prior ethical question constitutes a major flaw in John Stuart Mill's essay, *On Liberty*. Mill defends free expression on the basis of its social utility. Hocking states, "The whole point of the argument is not that intolerance infringes a right but that society is likely to lose by it. On this ground, the moment it can be shown that society stands to gain by intolerance Mill can have no word to say in behalf of liberty."[24] The individual would not have rights; he would have only such privileges as are consistent with the public welfare. "Thus we see in Mill the strange spectacle of a collectivist, in respect to method, arguing for individualism; the precise counterpart of Hobbes, an individualist in method arguing for collectivism."[25]

It is ironical, Hocking thinks, that the conception of rights as social functions is actually dysfunctional to social unity and vitality. This is because men in fact judge law by ethical standards. The condemnation of an innocent Dreyfus in order to save the prestige of a military class therefore did not really contribute to the social welfare. As knowledge of injustice "becomes a part of the consciousness of the community, a definite damage is done to the confidence of that community in the working of its own law."[26] Some proponents of the functional view also say that rights cannot be determined substantively, that they must be settled in specific situations by a disinterested spectator. But Hocking argues that impartiality is not sufficient. Such a judging party could not articulate human rights unless he was attempting to be just, and he could have no idea of what justice requires without a conception of rights.[27]

[22] "Ways of Thinking About Rights," p. 252.
[23] *Ibid.*, pp. 253-55.
[24] *LEI*, p. 83.
[25] *Ibid.*
[26] *PLR*, p. 51.
[27] "Justice, Law, and the Cases," pp. 241-44.

The final reason why Hocking rejects the functional view of rights is that the functions individuals could possibly perform are not known. They are not known because the potentialities of a person are never completely grasped, not even by the individual himself. Rights could not therefore be formulated simply in terms of current human capacities to perform present social functions.[28] An adequate conception of rights must be presumptive in nature.

PRESUMPTIVE RIGHT AND SOCIAL DUTY

Because he finds serious problems with the dominant ways of thinking about rights, Hocking seeks a sounder approach. He clears the ground by discussing the general characteristics of a claim to rights. He finds that the claim is a special sort of statement, very different from the claim to interests. The claim to rights is accompanied by an expectation of public support for the claim, but when one claims his interests he can expect no support for the attainment of his desires. And while one is free to relinquish his claim to an interest, he is not free to give up his claim to a right. A right has an element of duty implicit within it, "for by a peculiar logic within the claim of right, what I claim for myself I also claim for others similarly placed; hence what I relinquish for myself I relinquish also for them."[29] Since the claim to a right implies the attribution of the right to others, the claimant must accept the duty to respect a similar claim by others.[30] The claim to rights also cannot be unconditional.[31] A claim would be unconditional if no reasons were given to justify it. Reasons specify the circumstances under which the claim is made; the grounds for the claim vanish if the reasons are inadequate. But in spite of these restrictions inherent in the claim to rights, individuals are not necessarily stifled: "Men are less limited in solitude than in a dense society; but they are also less free for most of the significant objects of living."[32]

Hocking begins his substantive conception of rights by arguing that men must have a right to be treated by legal systems "as if" they were

[28] *PLR*, pp. 68-71.
[29] "On the Present Position of the Theory of Natural Right," p. 557.
[30] *LEI*, p. 55.
[31] *FP*, p. 73.
[32] *FP*, p. 67. Hocking repeats the widely accepted observation that although the claim to rights generally contains a demand for freedom, freedom either to be removed from restraint or to have the means to take some positive action, a person's freedom is limited by the freedom of others. For example, the freedom to decide one's life's work can only be partly satisfied in any given society, since the free choice of work must not constrain those who do not want its products. See *ibid.*, p. 66.

alike. There must be a "presumption" of equality. Only distinctions relevant to the purposes of law can be made if human rights are not to be violated.[33] For example, whether a man pays his debts has nothing to do with his weight, color, or family tree. Where, however, a distinction between people is markedly relevant to a right or a duty, law should recognize the distinction. The presumption of equality usually is withheld, for instance, in the case of people, such as minors or lunatics, who are not capable of forming a judgment in their own interest. Human rights are thus to a certain extent comparative. One person deserves the same as another if they are equal in all relevant ways.

The rights which can be claimed against government are presumptive in another sense: they are *creative* presumptions. Creative presumptions are those "imputed to individuals, and addressed to potentialities which are even now resident in them, in the deeper strata of their natures."[34] Since the purpose of the state is to further the individual's will to power, legal rights cannot be based simply on present capacities. The presumption of equality may be contrary to present reality; yet, the presumption will tend to create the equality presumed. For example, the presumption that men are equally fit to vote is not literally accurate, but it will tend to bring about that equal fitness.[35] Human rights are therefore "not primarily a set of conditions which promote the performance of functions; but a set of conditions which *promote the development of powers*."[36] The general principle may be formulated in this manner: "*It is objectively 'right' that an individual should develop his powers, whatever they are. This objective right is the true standard for legal right.*"[37]

For Hocking the concept of "natural right" has its only acceptable meaning in this right of the individual to develop his powers. "He may be said to have a 'natural right' to become what he is capable of becoming. This is his only natural right."[38] Of course, the implementation of this one natural right may require certain more specific rights. He suggests several.[39] For example, under most circumstances, there should be a "right to use one's own ideas in governing one's

---

[33] *PLR*, pp. 58-60.
[34] *Ibid.*, p. 67.
[35] He gives another example from everyday experience: "It aids a boy to reach maturity to treat him as if he were a little older than he is. A little older: for the presumption loses its effect if it is too wide of the actual fact." See *ibid.*, pp. 62-63.
[36] *Ibid.*, p. 71.
[37] *Ibid.*, pp. 71-72.
[38] *Ibid.*, p. 74.
[39] *Ibid.*, pp. 86-88.

undertakings." This would require, first, the "right of self-manage-ment," the right of the individual to grow through "making his own choices of occupation, residence, companions, in working out his own practices in manners and morals, and in so doing making his own ex-periments and mistakes." Second, there should be the "*right of liberty in seeking social control.*" The individual must have the right to persuade others to accept his ideas. Third, there should be the "*right of liberty in the control of nature.*" Because the use of things is necessary for personal development, the right to the ownership of property should be guar-anteed.

Although the individual has a natural right to self-development, Hocking argues that the claim to this right must be accompanied by "moral ambition," a "good will." This means, in part, that the indivi-dual "can suspend, and perhaps ultimately destroy his own right, by his own free choice not to become what he is capable of becoming."[40] Human powers do not develop without "moral ambition," and with-out a "good will" the claim to rights may hinder the development of the potentialities of others.[41] But even though an ill will removes the justification for the claim to rights, Hocking thinks society should be cautious in attributing an ill will to a person. Society should presume that moral ambition is present as long as it has the resources to help activate this motivation.[42]

In making the "good will" integral to the claim to rights, he realizes that an adequate theory cannot divorce the individual's rights from his community responsibilities. Hocking's approach to human nature and development, discussed above, supports such a conception of rights. The individual has the right and responsibility to develop his own potentialities, and he also has a duty to fulfill his "task as member of an historical community."[43] In fact, "there is but one stuff of which 'right' is made; the claim of the growing self to grow, to become what it is capable of becoming, *in the exchange of thought and help among fellow beings.*"[44] A person claiming the right to develop his will to power must therefore accept both his need for life in community and the legitimate claims of others to self-fulfillment. He "has a right to his *own share of the cost of satisfaction.*"[45] Hocking acknowledge that his approach to

[40] *Ibid.*, pp. 74-75.
[41] *Ibid.*, pp. 55, 73.
[42] *Ibid.*, p. 75.
[43] "On the Present Position of the Theory of Natural Right," p. 558.
[44] "History and the Absolute," pp. 450-51 (emphasis added).
[45] "Justice, Law, and the Cases," p. 347.

rights assumes that society will benefit from the development of the potentialities of its members.[46] It is an assumption that he believes is a central and acceptable premise of traditional liberalism. And because his theory of rights is the foundation for his approach to political limits and to political duty, it is crucial to his reformulation of liberalism.

THE REFORMULATION OF LIBERALISM

It is not the role of the political philosopher to discuss the political institutions and practices of particular societies. But a political philosophy gains in both comprehensiveness and persuasiveness if it helps us understand the assumptions and characteristic modes of thought that dominate our political life. Political philosophy should help us see the strengths and inadequacies of our ideological presuppositions. Hocking constantly related his philosophy to the attitudes and styles of thought that affect the actual operation of political institutions. He correctly thought that public policy "has its springs in the convictions and purposes of a people."[47] He applied his conception of human nature and his general theory of the political community and individual rights to the politically relevant thought patterns of the modern West, giving special attention to the United States.

The Great Depression of the 1930's constituted not only an economic crisis, but an intellectual crisis as well. The assumptions which had governed political thought and action were shaken. This crisis was, particularly in the United States, a crisis in liberalism, for liberalism was the reigning political ideology. Hocking wanted to discover those elements of liberalism which should be maintained and those which must be abandoned if societies were to solve their pressing problems. In 1935 he participated in a symposium on "The Future of Liberalism" sponsored by the American Philosophical Association. His address, along with those of the other two participants, John Dewey and C. E. Montague, was published in the *Journal of Philosophy*. His views were expanded in the Mahlon Powel Lectures at the University of Indiana in 1936, lectures which were published as *The Lasting Elements of Individualism*.

He recognizes that the core of Western liberalism is individualism; its dominant value is individual freedom. Although he gives much attention to the history of modern individualism, his interpretations are

[46] *PLR*, pp. 73-74.
[47] *SMN*, p. 12.

largely derivative and may be summarized quite briefly. He shows that liberalism has drawn heavily on natural rights theory, and he acknowledges his indebtedness to Maine's conception of the development of societies from status to contractual relationships. He suggests that the Reformation was important because of its emphasis on the person's obligation to think and believe for himself, subject to God alone. The Reformation saw individuality as "a continued living tension between various possibilities of belonging."[48] He thus cannot accept the suggestion that economic changes were the sole factor in the growth of modern individualism. The economic transformation of modern times was "merely the finishing touch in outlining the individual, whose mentality had already been essentially established. It is the shaking of the pod, which separates the ripened peas, and lets them fall out separate."[49] Men could not have begun to act in a self-sufficient manner unless they had started to think of themselves as self sufficient. Nevertheless, certain economic changes were important. For example, the scarcity of labor, beginning with the Black Death in the fourteenth century, caused active bidding for labor. Men were able to consider the question, "Whose man shall I be?" Since workers began to associate first with one employer and then with another, they ceased to identify with any one employer. The individual could then participate in a plurality of groups, and this, in turn, helped him to see himself as a distinct identity.[50]

Hocking realizes that the fundamental attitude underlying liberalism is "confidence toward the undemonstrated powers of the units of society; it means a faith that the welfare of any society may be trusted to the individuals who compose it."[51] Moreover, liberalism has insisted that the individual is, in fact, the ultimate unit of society. "And all of the life, all of the intelligence, all of the energy which they have derives ultimately from him. He is the generating focus out of which they are born."[52] Understood in this way, individualism is basic to the "liberal spirit," and should be preserved. But in spite of its underlying truth, Hocking thinks liberalism had hardened into an individualism so extreme that the foundations of political community were undercut and the capacities of political institutions to solve social and economic problems were vitiated. He believes we must distinguish be-

[48] *LEI*, p. 23. For the historical development of individualism, see pp. 1-36.
[49] *Ibid.*, p. 26.
[50] *Ibid.*, pp. 27-32.
[51] *Ibid.*, p 5.
[52] *Ibid.*, p. 4.

tween "a sound individualism and certain unsound counterfeits."[53]

By the early decades of this century, Hocking writes, liberalism had developed three basic weaknesses. One failure was the separation of the claim to rights from the acceptance of duties. Liberalism had adhered to the natural rights position so strongly that community responsibilities were almost completely forgotten. It was but a short step from an inalienable right to "a *privilege*, privilege being that specific virus which the liberal revolutions set themselves to destroy."[54] Another failure of liberalism was its "emotional defect." Liberalism had encouraged the development of self-confident men who cannot be trusted with power or wealth. They cannot be trusted, not because of their greatness, but because of their mediocrity. In its excessive individualism, liberalism had stressed freedom to the exclusion of personal excellence. "To say that each man is as good as the next means only that the next is as poor sort as the first." A mental climate was created in which men will no longer fight for the valid principles of liberalism; "liberalism has ceased to beget liberals."[55]

The third and most important weakness Hocking finds in traditional liberalism is its failure to achieve social unity. Liberalism had originally inherited some unifying habits of mind from feudalism, but extreme individualism had pulverized society.[56] There are several dimensions to this loss of unity. Politically, because it realized that power had been abused, liberalism sought to limit government by various institutionalized "checks and balances." But liberalism forgot that governmental power can be put to good as well as evil purposes. It distracted "the strong flow of political life" into "a delta of marshy trickles." Political institutions were therefore unable to act forcefully to solve those social and economic problems that cause disunity. Political action also contributes to social unity by encouraging an emotional interdependence between the citizens. An "active program and a common emotion of assent are inseparable."[57] A "common mind" among the people depends on common action, and common action needs to be both purposive and conscious. "For emotion can only exist when there

---

[53] *Ibid.*, pp. 6-7.

[54] *Ibid.*, p. 55.

[55] *Ibid.*, p. 59. It is obvious that there was a deep toughness in Hocking's character and thought. Several times in his writings he quotes Nietzsche's statement that "the will of all love is, the beloved one to *create*. And all creators are hard." See *LEI*, p. 63; *Experiment in Education*, pp. 162-63.

[56] *LEI*, pp. 41-42.

[57] *Ibid.*, p. 112.

is a consciousness of what we are doing, and for what end."[58] This purposive, conscious action is facilitated through political institutions; the common deeds of the political community *"help a common mind into being."*[59]

Hocking thinks disunity was also furthered by the economic assumptions of traditional liberalism. Liberalism did not encourage private reservoirs of wealth to have "any regular working-relations to the public concerns." It assumed that the sum total of all successful business enterprises would add up to an economically healthy nation. In actuality, they "constitute rather a set of prosperous spots, like pimples of prosperity on a visage predominately pale. They do not add themselves into the General Health."[60] It is not true that "total prosperity is made by multiplying individual prosperity."[61] Hocking's position is correct. Individual prosperity, though widespread, can co-exist with serious economic problems that will ultimately threaten that prosperity.

Hocking also rejects the assumption of traditional liberalism that the individual has an absolute natural right to use his property as he chooses. Any system of private property must rather "be subject to the judgment of its yield in human uses, and especially of its building of cultures and of men."[62] He suggests that since it is individual needs which industry should serve, the "totality of persons in a community who have a right to consume" should "determine what is produced."[63] It is thus the business of society, acting through government, to identify rightful demand and turn it into actual demand. What is needed are "new organs for transmitting demand."[64] Even Marxists often miss

[58] *Ibid.*, p. 152.
[59] *MATS*, p. 164.
[60] *LEI*, p. 48
[61] *Ibid.*
[62] *SWP*, p. 523. It is now often suggested that Western man must adopt an attitude of reverence for nature if we are to solve our massive problems of environmental pollution. Hocking makes a relevant point. In 1932, before it was a popular position, he defended the right of colonies to their independence. He rejects the contention that "advanced" Western nations have a right to dominate societies which do not "make use" of their resources. There are, he argues, a variety of "uses" for resources, and each makes valuable contributions to the development of human consciousness. The man in the "backward" society is "using his landscape, forest, rivers, running his habits through them, feeding his imagination on them, mixing his rude piety with them." Western man mistakenly believes that such raw materials are untouched and idle; we do not see that they are used for "nothing except to produce a certain type of man." *Ibid.*, p. 521.
[63] *LEI*, p. 166.
[64] *Ibid.*, p. 168. Since Hocking does not specify the possible nature of these new organs, we do not know how he would implement his general goal. Perhaps governmental direction and approval of private business investment would be a possible means to this end. He also makes a suggestion that is not at all original: government must enforce fair competition between business units by establishing rules which business could not administer alone *Ibid.*, p. 164.

this point, he writes, because they tend to concentrate so much on production that they think equal distribution of existing production is the chief goal of social policy.[65]

It should be clear that Hocking wrote on liberalism mainly in the 1930's. Since then our understanding of liberalism has been altered. Hocking's call for more positive governmental action and for the abandonment of *laissez-faire* economic policies is compatible with our present understanding of liberalism. But there is another aspect of contemporary liberalism that Hocking found he could not accept. The earlier liberalism had pictured the competition between individuals like the collision of atoms in a social void.[66] But contemporary American liberalism has adopted the voluntarist style of pluralism so extensively that Lowi refers to the "new public philosophy" of "interest-group liberalism." Lowi states that this new liberalism "sees as both necessary and good that the policy agenda and the public interest be defined in terms of the organized interests in society."[67] This liberalism thinks economic and political conflict occurs between groups, not individuals, and the balancing of group forces is relied on for social stability. In his final book, published in 1959, Hocking writes that the free competition of self-interested groups does not bring social unity, and it "has no inherent tendency to produce justice."[68] The result is "a radical weakness, an incapacity for sacrifice and self-restraint in the pursuit of that good-of-the-whole which, through defect of habit, has lost its place as first premise of our action."[69]

Hocking never abandoned the central commitment of liberalism, the belief in the uniqueness and inherent worth of the individual. Liberalism has insited that if the minds and consciences of citizens are constricted, the mental and moral life of the political community will be curtailed. The unity and common action of the political order can rest on the free commitments of its members "only when public purposes are prolongations of individual purposes."[70] Hocking also consistently argues that modern societies require a reformulated liberalism, a liberalism stressing individual development within the

[65] Hocking states that Marx's ethical emphasis on the right of the worker to the product of his work is more profound than the shallow claims of rights in liberalism, precisely because the right of the laborer is earned. *Ibid.*, p. 90.
[66] See Louis Hartz, *The Liberal Tradition in America* (New York: Harcourt, Brace & World, Inc , 1955), pp. 3-86.
[67] Lowi, *The End of Liberalism, op. cit.*, p 71.
[68] *SMN*, pp. 91-96.
[69] *Ibid.*, pp. 117-18.
[70] *LEI*, p. 133.

context of common political action and the fulfillment of community responsibilities. Liberalism's emphasis on the ultimate significance of the human being is not incompatible with the individual's "obligatory co-operation in an experimental program for an improved social order."[71]

POLITICAL PARTICIPATION AND LEADERSHIP

Liberalism has historically been a major force in encouraging the development of democratic institutions in the West.[72] Democracy involves "the spread of public power among the people"; it seeks to provide that "every man who is ruled is also a ruler."[73] Important liberal writings on democracy, such as Rousseau's *Social Contract* and John Stuart Mill's essay on *Representative Government*, had emphasized that democratic institutions could not function without high degrees of popular political participation and knowledge. Moreover, they assumed that political involvement was necessary to the development of the citizen's character and intellect.[74] But since World War II political scientists and sociologists have used voting data and the techniques of survey research to discover that knowledge and participation are actually quite limited, even in a highly "developed" society such as the United States.[75] Moreover, even well informed citizens may not partici-

---

[71] "The Future of Liberalism," p. 245.

[72] Most writers define Western liberal democracy in terms of these principles: popular sovereignty, or control by the people of governmental decisions through representative assemblies and electoral processes; political equality, or equal weight in voting; majority rule; and political freedom, which involves the right of expression and the right to organize political groups to oppose the regime in power. See, for example, Henry B. Mayo, *An Introduction to Democratic Theory* (New York: Oxford University Press, 1960), pp. 58-71.

[73] "Democracy and the Scientific Spirit," p. 432. Hocking agrees with the well-known justifications for democratic institutions. First, democracy brings security for the individuals of a society, since governors will not be likely to oppress citizens to which they are responsible for their offices. Second, a democracy is more likely to receive the support of the people than a non-democratic system, because the people will support to a higher degree those systems in which they participate most. Third, the education of the people will be furthered, for when people are trusted with power they become trained in its use. They will become more informed and more tolerant of the opinions of others as they participate in public discussion. Fourth, those who are obligated to live under a government have a moral right to a voice in its decisions. These four justifying principles are based on the assumption of "an underlying equality of mankind, among the obvious differences." This equality is not an equality of ability or intelligence, which anthropology, psychology, and sociology have questioned. "The equality which men need to have for democratic purposes is *not equality of fact, but equality of possibility, and especially equality of moral possibility.*" *Ibid.*, pp. 431-32.

[74] This assumption is discussed by Jack L. Walker, "A Critique of the Elitist Theory of Democracy," *The American Political Science Review* LX (June 1966), pp. 285-95, and Peter Bachrach, *The Theory of Democratic Elitism* (Boston: Little, Brown and Co., 1967), pp. 1-9.

[75] See the following: Bernard R. Berelson, Paul F. Lazarsfeld, and William N. McPhee, *Voting* (Chicago: University of Chicago Press, 1954); Seymour Martin Lipset, *Political Man*

pate rationally; they often use their knowledge simply to confirm their prejudices. Rather than conclude that Western societies like the United States do not function as democracies, these social scientists have revised the classical liberal idea of what democracy requires of citizens. Not only do they say that democracy can exist despite high levels of citizen non-involvement, but they even argue that a good deal of political apathy is actually desirable. They take this position largely because they are concerned primarily about the stability or "equilibrium" of the political system. They argue that a large number of apathetic citizens will provide a "cushion" for societal change. The non-involved will supposedly accept those small, incremental changes initiated by elites, and they will not themselves initiate extreme changes that might threaten the stability of the system. It is also assumed that apathy is necessary if the society is to have political leadership, that non-apathetic citizens will have difficulty following leaders. Almond and Verba write, "The need for elite power requires that the ordinary citizen be relatively passive, uninvolved, and deferential to elites."[76] The conclusion drawn by this approach is that a democratic political system requires a mixture of apathy and involvement, knowledge and ignorance, rationality and prejudice.[77]

Hocking is sympathetic to the types of concerns expressed by these writers, but he does not believe apathy is either necessary or desirable for a democratic system. He does think that our traditional conception of democracy is misguided when it insists that "the citizens, as equals, are all supposed to be equally interested in all phases of the state."[78] This is impossible in complex modern societies, and it obscures the need for leadership. But this realization does not lead Hocking to support apathy. It causes him to seek instead a more adequate conception of political involvement. If the political order is to fulfill its purpose, Hocking thinks each citizen must focus on the contribution he can make to the common life. The robust political community will be characterized by a style of participation in which "the contribution of the individual is chiefly along the line of his own special interest and capacity."[79] Although he does not mention sources, Hocking is applying to modern democracies the conception of political participation

(Garden City, New York: Doubleday and Co., Inc., 1963), pp. 183-300; and Lester W. Milbrath, *Political Participation* (Chicago: Rand McNally, 1965).

[76] Gabriel A. Almond and Sidney Verba, *The Civic Culture* (Boston: Little, Brown and Co., 1965), p. 343.

[77] Berelson, Lazarsfeld, and McPhee, *op. cit.*, ch. 14.

[78] *LEI*, p. 157.

[79] *Ibid.*

held by classical political philosophy. Plato and Aristotle had argued that individual happiness and political health require that each individual perform those functions for which he is best suited. Hocking thinks that if this type of involvement were to permeate democratic institutions, the political order would be a "co-agent state."

He derives this concept of the "co-agent state" from the ordinary human experience in which one person becomes the "agent" of another. The responsible agent may make subordinate decisions in carrying out the will of the principal (the authorizing person), but he should both understand the desires of the principal and agree to execute those desires. The principal has not decided *what* the agent decides, but he has decided *that* the agent decides. Thus, the decisions of the agent are also the decisions of the principal.[80] Likewise, in the democratic political order, the citizen "does not know how to solve the legal issue nor the engineering problem; but he is concerned that they be solved." It is "this original stock of purpose which constitutes the governmental deed the work of a responsible agent of the citizen, so that its deeds are *ipso facto* his deeds, the extrapolation of his will."[81] The decisions as to means are made by the governmental agents, in order to accomplish the ends desired by the citizens.

This approach to political participation emphasizes the compatibility between leadership and democratic institutions. As shown in Chapter II, Hocking thinks the term-making and commotive aspects of politics both require leadership. Conflict settlements and common commitments must be proposed and assent to them won. But adequate leadership is not based on citizen apathy. It depends, Hocking argues, on positive support of leaders by citizens, support that is evoked when leaders call the people to common purposes and action. The function of the leader is, "without being alien to any popular feeling, and without following it – to reflect it, to reflect upon it, to mix it with thought, inform it, and direct it."[82] Effective leadership also places responsibility on the leader as well as on the citizen. The successful democratic leader must call "for corroboration from the certitudes of his own neighbors."[83] He leads not by power but by strength, "a strength *with* others – a mental-moral relation implying some community of goal: in this relation, the more strength the less need to

[80] *Ibid.*, p. 143-44.
[81] *Ibid.*, p. 147.
[82] "Leaders and Led," pp. 633-34.
[83] *SMN*, p. 195.

bring into play power or the threat of power."[84] Such strength contains an element of command, but it is a type of command which "makes the We-will the essence of each I-will."[85]

When he discusses the personal qualities of leaders, Hocking reformulates the conception of authority held by traditional liberalism. Liberalism had historically sought to free men from the personal authority of feudal and monarchical rule. Personal authority was thought to be capricious and arbitrary; impersonal authority was assumed to be rational and impartial. Today, however, there are an increasing number of attacks on impersonal authority, especially bureaucratic authority.[86] Hocking states that if leaders are to win the support of citizens to common political actions and purposes, they must personally embody the values they recommend. He also believes it is possible to specify those personal characteristics that are generally desirable in the democratic leader.[87]

Adequate conceptions of leadership and political participation will, Hocking thinks, also show that effective leadership is compatible with dissent and popular criticism. Although the responsible citizen must see that his own fulfillment requires that he contribute to the common life, he must at the same time be critical of the actions of public officials. Liberalism has rightly emphasized that in the sound political order the citizen must judge the success or failure of governmental policies. The state must never attempt to "enforce unanimity of opinion as to the wisdom or success of these measures. It must submit its experiment from moment to moment to the judgment of free judges, as guide to the next experimental stage."[88] The healthy government will strive to develop citizens of strong conscience and conviction, men who are inwardly free enough to be critical, and it will provide "sedulously for an honest and competent opposition."[89] Hocking devoted considerable attention to the general problem of free expression, both

[84] *Ibid.*, p. 167.
[85] *Ibid.*, p. 172.
[86] For example, see Schaar, *op. cit.*, pp. 302-08.
[87] He lists these characteristics ("Leaders and Led," p. 634):
"First,. . . integrity, justice, and an eye single to public welfare;
  Second, the amalgamating virtues, such as bring about a sentiment of solidarity and loyalty within the group, make a mental entity of neighborhood and community, realize the family aspect of the state, create the conviction of mutuality of lot in the commonwealth;
  Third, the actualizing virtues, such as bring decisions to pass out of confused deliberations, keep public business going. . . .
  Fourth, vision, the outlook and sense of direction of the statesmen. . . ."
[88] *LEI*, p. 135.
[89] *Ibid.*, p. 177.

because of its political significance and because of its crucial role in the development of the individual's will to power. His approach to free expression merits extended consideration.

THE FREEDOM OF EXPRESSION

Hocking had the opportunity to give his sustained attention to the problem of free expression during his service on the Commission on Freedom of the Press, an independent commission operating under a grant of funds by Time, Inc., and Encyclopedia Britannica, Inc., to the University of Chicago. Although *Freedom of the Press: A Framework of Principle* (1947) was published by the commission, it is Hocking's personal statement.[90] His goal is the formulation of an approach that will relate free expression to the rights of the individual and to the requirements of community.

Freedom of expression has been a hallmark of liberalism. John Stuart Mill's essay, *On Liberty*, perhaps the most famous statement of the liberal view of expression, is well known. Mill argued that in the absence of infallibility, all ideas should be freely expressed, including those which are true, those which are half-true, and those which are altogether false. Suppression of true ideas will hinder social progress, and the suppression of ideas which are partially or totally false will deny citizens the opportunity to learn why they hold their ideas and why they are true or false.[91] One of the disagreements between liberalism and political conservatism is over the question of free expression. Conservatism often assumes that traditional institutions and values must be protected from threatening forms of expression. The conservative also sometimes accuses the liberal of supporting free expression simply because of a skepticism toward the possibility of knowing truth.[92]

Mill's argument that the social welfare requires the right to free expression has been accepted by later liberals, including many Americans who support an absolutist interpretation of the First Amendment to the United States Constitution.[93] Hocking agrees that

[90] Throughout the book there are footnotes containing comments or objections by other members of the commission and Hocking's replies. Although this work has the word "press" in its title, he states that he uses the term in a broad sense to refer to communication through "book, magazine, radio, film, etc." See p. 162.

[91] See *on Liberty*, ch. II.

[92] See Willmoore Kendall, "The 'Open Society' and Its Fallacies," in *Limits of Liberty*, ed. by Peter Radcliff (Belmont, Calif.: Wadsworth Publishing Co., Inc., 1966), pp. 27-42.

[93] See, for example, Alexander Meiklejohn, *Free Speech and Its Relation to Self-Government* (New York: Harper and Brothers, 1948).

since social vitality requires that citizens create and share new ideas, society can have no long term interest in repressing expression. But he believes that if free expression is to be securely founded, it must be a right of the individual rather than a privilege granted by society for social ends. Free expression should be a right because it is necessary for self-development and for sociality. "Whatever is so intimately bound up with mental existence and normal growth as expression is may reasonably be regarded as a part of that freedom which a man not only does claim as an interest but ought to claim as a right, for himself and also for others."[94] Each person has a double duty: he should protect the freedom of expression of other members of society, and he must express his own thought.[95]

Hocking also rejects the liberal assumption of the "self-righting character of public discussion," the notion that expression should be free because free competition between ideas brings to dominance the best ideas. John Milton stated this position in classic form, taking his image of the competition among ideas from the jousting meet. He contends that when truth and falsehood struggle, truth will emerge victorious if there is a free and open encounter.[96] Another famous statement of this approach is contained in United States Supreme Court Justice Oliver Wendell Hollmes' image of the marketplace: " 'The best test of truth is the power of thought to get itself accepted in the competition of the market.' "[97] This approach assumes that variety among the contesting ideas and freedom in the contest itself will "favor the validity of the resulting choice";[98] it assumes there is a struggle for survival among ideas in which a process of natural selection occurs.[99]

Hocking finds several weaknesses in this free competition argument.[100] First, the tournament image is not appropriate, because ideas often do not encounter each other in a genuine struggle. For example, citizens may not consider ideas critical of their own, and the press often does not present a diversity of ideas. Second, the truth will in all likeli-

---

[94] *FP*, p. 96.
[95] *Ibid.*, p. 97.
[96] Hocking quotes Milton (*FP*, p. 13):
" '*Though all the winds of doctrine were let loose to play upon the earth, so Truth be in the field, we do injuriously by licensing and prohibiting to misdoubt her strength. Let her and Falsehood grapple; who ever knew Truth put to the wors [sic] in a free and open encounter. Her confuting is the best and surest suppressing.*' "
[97] Quoted in *ibid.*, p. 107.
[98] *Ibid.*, p. 92.
[99] *Ibid.*, p. 13.
[100] *Ibid.*, pp. 14, 91-93.

hood not be among any of the contesting positions. Third, there is no end of the contest and no announcement of victory. Fourth and most serious, the "free competition" position omits any test of truth. According to that argument, truth cannot be known until the contest is over and the winning ideas are declared true. This amounts to "The winner always wins," a statement which says nothing. Hocking is correct; truth does not inevitably emerge from the competition between ideas. If truth is to result, the proponents of ideas must genuinely seek truth. Hocking should have pointed out, but did not, that conflict between ideas is a necessary rather than a sufficient requirement for the emergence of truth. Such a position is implicit within his dialectical perspective on inquiry.

Hocking also rejects the liberal approach to toleration, because it is based on skepticism. He thinks real toleration is possible only when one believes he is in the presence of error. A person who has no commitments can hardly consider free expression to be important. "If we are caught in a complete antecedent incertitude or relativity of our minds in respect to truth, we must indeed be tolerant, but we reduce ourselves to bystanders in the struggle, we cease to fight, and free speech loses all interest in persuasion and all importance."[101] But Hocking does not go on to deny the importance of toleration. Instead, he offers a different argument for toleration. He insists that it is grounded not on ignorance of truth, but on respect for the right of others to make their own discovery of truth.[102] The wrong results of thought must be tolerated, since a person must discover his mistakes himself if truth is to be his own, rather than an imposed opinion.[103]

Hocking realizes that many limitations on free expression originate in social pressure rather than governmental action. He even suggests that ideas often arouse resistance in a measure proportionate to their significance. But he cannot accept Mill's argument that there should be no penalty whatsoever for the expression of opinion, that no social pressures should be exerted against the proponent of ideas. Hocking insists that Mill's prescription of "no penalty" for expression should be changed to "no irrelevant penalty."[104] Government should attempt to lift the level of social conflict from violence to discussion, but it should not try to eliminate all pressures against a person who expresses himself. The individual should be protected only from "types of harm *not*

---

[101] *Ibid.*, p. 107.
[102] *Ibid.*, p. 108.
[103] "Freedom of the Press in America," pp. 16-17.
[104] *LEI*, pp. 74-75

an integral part of the argument or relevant to the argument."[105] As an example
of relevant and irrelevant penalties, he states that Spinoza was rightly
excluded from the synagogue, since the thoughts he was expressing did
not warrant his being there; but it was wrong for the Jewish community
to attempt to ostracize him entirely, because this deprived him of the
power to express his ideas within that community and was an irrelevant penalty.[106]

There are two reasons why Hocking adopts this position. First, the
inevitable disapproval of strange ideas is a necessary condition for
the development of moral courage. "The right of freedom of speech
ought to be a right to the facilities for winning the ear of men in an
uphill fight, in the face of public disapproval."[107] Second, "to hold a
belief and not act on it out of consideration for the critics, is to become
supine and a moral jellyfish," and "to hold a belief and to act on it is
to pinch those who disagree."[108] The "normal destiny of an idea is to
come to some sort of power." Therefore, when an idea attains social
and political significance, opposing ideas must be discarded or rendered
powerless.[109]

Although free expression is an important individual right, Hocking
does not think it can be an absolute right. He suggests that the claim
to this right, like all claims to rights, must be accompanied by a good
will, a commitment to the truth and to the common good. He realizes
that it is very dangerous for government to determine whether the
claim to free expression is legitimate in specific cases. Officials will be
tempted to use their power in their own favor; the instruments available to government are incapable of fine discrimination between either
truth and falsehood or good and evil intent; and governmental inter-
vention may threaten the courage and spontaneity of the citizens.
Nevertheless, while caution is highly necessary, government must determine which general forms of expression are permissible.[110]

Government should restrain free expression only if people "are being
deceived, injured, or degraded by the manner in which others are
using their freedom to speak or print or show pictures."[111] Government
may limit expression which "*becomes equivalent to aggressive action.*"[112]

---

[105] *FP*, pp 100-01.
[106] *LEI*, pp. 75-78.
[107] *Ibid.*, p. 77.
[108] "The Meaning of Liberalism: An Essay in Definition," p. 50.
[109] *LEI*, p. 76.
[110] *FP*, pp. 114-16.
[111] *Ibid.*, p. 117. This paragraph is based on pp. 82-126.
[112] *Ibid.*, p. 126.

The major types of expression limited by law in the United States, for example, are libel and slander, obscenity and pornography, and expression encouraging sedition or disrupting the public order. Hocking argues that libel and slander constitute aggressive action because they injure the tangible personal interests of individuals. Although he states that obscenity threatens vulnerable standards of the community, he does not offer guidelines for distinguishing the obscene from art or social criticism. He simply suggests that the censor cannot operate effectively in this area unless he has the conscience of the community behind him.[113] And in his late writing he is quite pessimistic about the capacity of government actually to limit obscene materials. If the state draws such a line and tries to police it, "it will in all probability pile up publicity along the border and make the regulation ridiculous. What experience seems to show is that both censorship and no-censorship are failures: stalemate!"[114]

Seditious expression is aggressive in nature, Hocking writes, because it threatens the general security. Since it is in everyone's interest that there be a stable political order, the freedom of expression of some may be limited to protect the total freedom of the community.[115] Expression can be assumed to be seditious when "the country is so far disturbed that a talk revolution tends to become an actual revolution."[116] This position might not seem compatible with another statement: "The state cannot limit the diversity of philosophy even though it appear to undermine the state's foundations; it must give free play to every effort to persuade."[117] Hocking is suggesting that there must be rather complete freedom to advocate any position on the philosophical level, but that advocacy that tends to bring harmful action may not be allowed. This is roughly the same position later adopted by the United States Supreme Court in *Yates vs. U.S.*[118] But there is a problem with this distinction between philosophical advocacy and advocacy to action. Hocking always insists that ideas are important because people act on them. Indeed, those who do not so act are accused of cowardice and flabbiness of character. He would have

---

[113] *Ibid.*, p. 82.
[114] *CWC*, p. 14.
[115] *FP*, p. 125. A society committed to free expression is in particular peril, Hocking writes: For "liberalism is steeped in paradox: Shall the liberal be liberal also to the illiberal? If its principle is universal, it must be. But on the other hand the opposition is not prevented by its own principles from moving to annihilate liberalism." See "The Meaning of Liberalism," p. 49.
[116] *LEI*, p. 80.
[117] *MATS*, p. 442.
[118] 355 U.S. 66 (1957).

strengthened his argument had he directly discussed this problem and precisely specified the types of expression that are seditious. His approach to governmental limitations of expression is insufficiently developed.

Up to this point the question of free expression has centered around the right of the person who wishes to express his ideas. But in a society based on liberal democratic institutions the right of the listener is also important. The citizens of a democracy have a right to ideas and information because they must judge the affairs of the nation and the world in a time when "world public order" may depend on events which occur thousands of miles away.[119] There is a new right, "*the right of the public to adequacy and truth in the news.*" This right implies a corresponding duty on the part of the organizations of mass communication. They should have no freedom "to lie, to distort, to conceal truth, to misrepresent issues, to malign motives of men and nations, to play on prejudices, to exaggerate emotions."[120] Ownership of organizations of mass communication should not confer the privilege of deafness toward ideas and information that need to be heard.[121] The people are not simply entitled to a free press; they also have a right to an adequate press. Leaders of the press should not lose their right to publish what they think, but they "*may lose the liberty' . . to fail* in the task of connecting the minds of their readers with the going currents of fact, thought, and feeling in the world of their membership."[122]

The organizations of mass communication are large commercial enterprises, Hocking writes, because modern technology requires mass production and great capital investment. The corporate nature of these organizations poses special problems to the right of the public for information and ideas.[123] There is a danger of monopoly that imperils the diversity of sources of public information.[124] Also, these enterprises are big businesses, closely interlocked with other financial and industrial organizations. They are therefore under the constant tempta-

---

[119] *LEI*, p. 76.

[120] "Freedom of the Press in America," p. 12.

[121] *FP*, pp. 98-99. The term, "organizations of mass communication," is within the broad scope Hocking attaches to the term, "press." See note 90, above. When this book was published, television was not yet socially important.

[122] *Ibid.*, pp. 187-88.

[123] Hocking believes the large scale nature of the mass communications media also poses a problem of free expression for the members of those organizations. Their voices are muffled by the hierarchical arrangement. He does not think that the freedom of expression of these members can be achieved without dissolving the organizations, and he does not support this, because society would thereby lose important sources of information. See *ibid.*, pp. 150-52.

[124] *Ibid.*, p. 156.

tion to favor those related institutions in their judgments and their presentation of information.[125]

Government should, Hocking thinks, have some responsibility in insuring that these organizations fulfill their public duty. A democratic government should not actually edit the news, for this would endanger the mental vitality of the people, and no set of office holders should be in a position to select the facts upon which their performance will be evaluated.[126] But government may act in other ways. Hocking calls attention to the decision of the United States Supreme Court in *United States vs. Associated Press*.[127] Because it refused to sell its services to certain newspapers, the Associated Press was found to be acting "in restraint of trade" in violation of the Sherman Antitrust Act. The reasoning in the case implies that whoever is in possession of information important to the public may be required to make that information publicly available.[128] Justices Black and Frankfurther stated, according to Hocking, that a public interest essential to democratic government should not be defeated by private restraints.[129] Hocking believes this decision amounts to the position that the press is "clothed by a public interest." He also argues that government should act in several other ways to encourage mass communications organizations to fulfill their public responsibilities: law should require the correction of any demonstrable falsehood, and the law of bribery should be expanded to prevent proven purchase of opinion or news statement, its penalty extending the removal of the guilty party from the practice of journalism.[130] He also suggests that government should aid private efforts to provide adequate news coverage outside the large metropolitan centers.[131]

[125] *Ibid.*, p. 196.
[126] *Ibid.*, p. 174.
[127] 326 U.S. 1 (1945).
[128] *FP*, p. 159.
[129] *Ibid.*, p. 172.
[130] *Ibid.*, pp. 187-88.
[131] *Ibid.*, p. 186. Hocking thinks that one of the basic shortcomings of American radio and television cannot be directly remedied by government action. In testimony submitted to Federal Communications Commission hearings in 1958 he argues that these media are characterized, especially in their advertising, by incessant, attention-assaulting forms off expression. And the entertainment they offer, so important to the "unintended education" of the public, favors the "animal end of the emotional scale." The only government involvement he suggests is the creation of a cabinet level officer for Fine Art to help "summon the American public to clearer judgments in this vital field where respected standards are more effective than legally enforceable definitions." But the basic remedy for this shortcoming is a higher degree of honor in these organizations, manifested in self-administered professional standards. See "Principles of Mass Communications by Radio and Television from the Angle of Philosophy and Psychology," 1959, especially pp. 3-4, 10-11. (Mimeographed.)

This chapter has shown how Hocking applies his philosophy of the political community to this dilemma: "You must have a genuine political life; yet you cannot have it at the cost of stultifying or regimenting individuals."[132] He offers a way past this dilemma with a comprehensive perspective on the individual's rights and his community responsibilities. He develops this perspective in a theory of human rights, a reformulation of liberalism, a conception of political participation and leadership, and an analysis of the freedom of expression. He thus gives his general political philosophy a concrete dimension by relating it to more specific problems of political thought. Although he can offer no final solutions, his theory will, if it is taken seriously, enable us to think more clearly about these problems.[133]

---

[132] *LEI*, p. 140.

[133] He does not think that political principles can contain fiinal recommendations concerning what should be done in specific political situations. Principles are necessary if we are to think about our problems, but principles must be properly understood. He writes ("Colonies and Dependent Areas," p. 17):

"The full meaning of any principle is not known until it is applied to particular cases. . . . In any concrete case, it is likely that more than one principle is pertinent, so that the attempt to judge by a single principle gives a one-sided or 'abstract' view. . . . The role of any principle is therefore to establish a presumption, not to dictate a final conclusion, about what ought to be or [not] be done."

CHAPTER V

LIBERTY AND COMMUNITY IN
INTERNATIONAL RELATIONS

Hocking realized that a general theory must not lose touch with particular facts. He thus self-consciously related his principles to "specific situations – which always refuse to accommodate themselves to the role of merely illustrating a theory."[1] International relations was one area in which he applied his political philosophy to concrete problems. In a number of writings, published over a period of fifty years, he considered this question: how can the liberty of each state to pursue its own "experiment in living" be compatible with community in the relations between states? It would be impossible to summarize Hocking's wide travels and his extensive writings on international relations. Some of the more important are mentioned in the introduction.[2] A man who took his citizen responsibilities seriously, he expressed his convictions on a broad range of international issues, from famine in Asia to the intellectual challenges posed by nuclear weapons. These views were presented not only in books and articles, but also in addresses, letters to the editor, and radio discussions. A sense of the range of his interests and felt responsibilities may be gained from a glance at his selected bibliography. It is not necessary to this study that all his writings on international relations be discussed. Many were

[1] *SWP*, pp. vii-viii.
[2] Hocking's most important book in the area of international relations is *The Spirit of World Politics*. It received quite favorable reviews when it appeared in 1932. Henry K. Norton stated that it consists of two parts:
"One a most thought-provoking philosophical examination of the bases of our international assumptions, and the other an excellent analysis of the actual operation of imperialism in Egypt, Syria, and Palestine. . . . No student of world politics can well consider his equipment complete or his preparation adequate who has not read, pondered and digested this volume."
See *Saturday Review*, July 30, 1932, p. 15. In *The New Republic*, July 13, 1932, pp. 239-40, Raymond Leslie Buell wrote, "Professor Hocking's discussion of nationalism and imperialism is both brilliant and profound – quite the best which this reviewer has seen." For another favorable reaction see Rupert Emerson's review in *The American Political Science Review*, XXVI (August, 1932), pp. 745-47.

topical, limited in significance to a specific time and a narrow issue. Those are considered that are particularly relevant to the role of ethics in international affairs and to the problem of securing international peace.

ETHICS AND INTERNATIONAL RELATIONS

Are ethical standards that are appropriate for personal morality applicable to the relations between states? This has been an old question in political thought. During the past several decades this argument has been important to what is often called the "realist-idealist" controversy.[3] The "idealist" position assumes that the basic principles of personal morality in the Western tradition can be immediately and directly applied in international affairs. Hocking summarizes the four principles of the "Kantian-Christian" ethical tradition.[4] The first principle is justice or impartiality, which requires debt-paying, promise-keeping, and application of the same standards of judgment to great and small, friend and foe. The second principle, forbearance or patience, is "a disposition not so much to endure evil as to give due scope to the self-corrective process of the other mind." The third principle, forgiveness, requires one to refrain from punishing another and to resume friendly relations after a breach of loyalty by the other. The fourth principle is non-resistance or self-sacrifice. Some who believe that these principles can be applied to international relations advocate the creation of some form of world government to replace organizations of sovereign states like the United Nations.[5] Others who accept the "idealist" position concentrate on the goal of disarmament. Some of them are more optimistic about the possibilities of disarmament now that peace is based on a balance of nuclear terror. Walter Millis thinks, for example, that "the military establishments will progressively decline into forces policing, through their defensive roles, a more or less established world order, while international politics advances to the generally nonviolent regulation and adjustment of the power struggles that will continue to take place in it."[6]

The "realist" position was well-stated by Thucydides in his *History of the Peloponnesian War*. The Athenian ambassadors to Melos announce:

---

[3] For a general discussion of this controversy, see John H. Herz, *Political Realism and Political Idealism* (Chicago: University of Chicago Press, 1951).

[4] *SWP*, pp. 479-80.

[5] See, for example, Grenville Clark and Louis B. Sohn, *World Peace Through World Law* (Cambridge, Mass.: Harvard University Press, 1962).

[6] *An End to Arms* (New York: Atheneum, 1965), p. 226.

"Right, as the world goes, is only in question between equals in power, while the strong do what they can and the weak suffer what they must."[7] This view admits that standards of justice or benevolence may be appropriate for interpersonal relations, since states are able to provide minimal order and security. But the realist position insists that moral standards cannot be directly applied in international affairs, because of the lack of international order and the experienced insecurity of every state. Each state simply does what it must to protect itself.

Hans Morgenthau has been the leading academic exponent of the realist position.[8] He writes that the "main signpost that helps political realism to find its way through the landscape of international politics is the concept of interest defined in terms of power."[9] Every nation, he argues, must protect its security through traditional balance of power diplomacy and the maintenance of military and economic strength. For "as long as the world is politically organized into nations, the national interest is indeed the last word in international politics."[10] Morgenthau has been criticized for minimizing the possible role of morality in international relations. Tannenbaum is probably excessive when he claims that "this doctrine is confessedly, nay gleefully amoral."[11] Brandon states, "*Virtú* for Machiavelli, prudence for Morgenthau, consists in doing what reason requires for the selfish ends of the state, and is not in fact connected with any moral principles above the narrow pursuit of national power and security."[12] Brandon criticizes Morgenthau for not stressing "the obligation of men and nations to attempt to improve international relations and to try to realize greater freedom, justice, and order in world affairs."[13]

Hocking attempts to formulate an approach to this problem of

[7] *The Complete Writings of Thucydides: The Peloponnesian War* (New York: The Modern Library, 1951), p. 331.

[8] See especially "Another 'Great Debate': The National Interest of the United States," *The American Political Science Review*, XLVI (December 1952), pp. 961-88; *In Defense of the National Interest* (New York: Alfred A. Knopf, Inc., 1951); and *Politics Among Nations* (3rd edition, New York: Alfred A. Knopf, Inc., 1960).

[9] *Politics Among Nations, op. cit.*, p. 5. Morgenthau argues that the application of universal moral principles is likely to result in the ideological identity of those principles with imperial desires, as in the American expansionist period of Presidents McKinley and Theodore Roosevelt, or the subordination of real national interests to moral principles, as occurred under President Woodrow Wilson. See "The Primacy of the National Interest," *The American Scholar*, XVIII (Spring, 1949), pp. 207-10.

[10] *Dilemmas of Politics* (University of Chicago Press, 1958), p. 62.

[11] Frank Tannenbaum, "The Balance of Power vs. The Coordinate State," *Political Science Quarterly*, LXVII (June, 1952), p. 173.

[12] Donald Brandon, *American Foreign Policy: Beyond Utopianism and Realism* (New York: Appleton-Century-Crofts, 1966), p. 93.

[13] *Ibid.*, p. 90.

ethics in international relations that will neither absolve states of moral responsibility nor fail to take account of the peculiar circumstances of international relations. The ethical principles of the western tradition do apply to states, he argues. States are not, of course, persons, as the older legal fiction would have it, but they are composed of individual moral agents. Individuals cannot be excused by the claim that they act on behalf of states, and states cannot claim that their actions are not actions of individuals.[14] Hocking also realizes, however, that the "Kantian-Christian" moral standards cannot be simply, directly applied to state behavior.[15] Unlike some realists, he does not rely on descriptions of human evil and the inevitably corrupting nature of political power to explain why ethical principles are so hard to apply. He explains the difficulty in terms of peculiar conditions implicit in the nature of states and the arena of their interaction.[15] First, it is not easy to attribute responsibility for the actions of a previous regime to a present regime. When, for example, Russia repudiated the debts of the Czar, there was truth in the argument that the new regime did not incur them. The responsibility of a given group of leaders is also ambiguous, because leaders generally interpret "self-seeking on the part of states" as "altruism to its members actual and unborn."[17] And aggrandizement by states does often result in a better life for their members, providing the aggrandizement does not lead to conflicts so destructive as modern warfare. Second, there is often a tendency in the affairs of nations for the status quo to be accepted as just, and violations of the new status quo come to appear unjust. The irony is that although a new status quo may be disapproved, it may actually come to receive wider support than the old status quo ever had. "It is not true that the end justifies any means whatever, nor that the success of a *coup* makes it right; but it may be right for a state to assume the responsibility for establishing the new status (as in the Revolution of 1776) in advance of the general approval of mankind, and with that ultimate approval definitely in view."[18]

---

[14] *SWP*, pp. 470-74.

[15] He thinks the four principles are not equally susceptible of application to international relations. Justice is easier to apply than forbearance; forebearance can be applied more readily than forgiveness; forgiveness, in turn, is not so hard to act on as non-resistance or self-sacrifice. This last principle is so difficult to apply because it is generally effective only in direct personal relationships where "the language of feeling is direct," that is, where a creative emotional response is possible. Non-creative sacrifice, sacrifice which does not call the other back to his duties, is not even ethical. See *ibid.*, pp. 479-80.

[16] *Ibid.*, pp. 482-91.

[17] "Ethics and International Relations," p. 699.

[18] *SWP*, p. 485.

The third and most important factor limiting the direct application of personal morality is the uniqueness of states. "The whole complex situation of each state is so utterly incomparable with that of any other that each must do and have many things which no other can do or have."[19] State uniqueness vitiates that traditional concept of justice which insists that "one must treat equals equally, and unequals proportionately, that is, by equal measure."[20] He illustrates the problem by asking several rhetorical questions. Does Italy have a right to as many square miles per person as Canada? Does the United States have a right to include California? Does Russia have a right to access to the Mediterranean? It has become customary in international law and relations, he writes, to speak of questions dealing with the existence and extent of states as "nonjusticiable." This means that no state can afford to adhere to the judgments of other states or international legal organs in matters affecting its vital interests. It cannot do so because other parties are "unaware *through direct experience* of its unique requirements."[21] Moreover, the application of international law may even be unjust, Hocking declares. For example, when Iceland, a country poor in natural resources, declared a twelve-mile limit for its fisheries, Britain attempted to ignore the claim and relied on the traditional three mile limit of international law. Britain's legal rectitude was wrong by a standard of judgment which took Iceland's particular situation into account. Because "each national life has its own unique conditions, it must be its own judge as to what is necessary to its creative productivity."[22]

Although the principles of personal morality cannot be directly applied to international relations, Hocking insists that they may be indirectly applied through an interpretation of the nation as "*a specific experiment in living and law making.*"[23] Not only should each nation be free to express its own cultural identity, free from external domination, but each has much to learn from other national experiments. The nation, like the individual, develops through mutual criticism as it confronts other ways of life. Each is "*culturally pregnant*, has something to say through its arts, institutions, laws, which all civilized mankind [should] want to hear."[24] The desire of a people for national experi-

[19] *Ibid.*, p. 482.
[20] *Ibid.*, p. 483.
[21] *Ibid.*, p. 182.
[22] "The Spiritual Effect of Warlessness," p. 152.
[23] *SMN*, p. 100. The term "nation" is discussed in Chapter III, note 76, above.
[24] *EE*, p. 210.

mentation is quite different from "national egoism," or what is often called "nationalism." National egoism, Hocking writes, is the attitude that nothing can be learned from other national experiments. It has as a likely result not only conflict but also a general impoverishment, the same effect personal egoism has on individuals.[25]

Hocking suggests several "theorums" that would, if followed, indirectly lead to a partial application of the principles of the Western moral tradition to the relations between states. First, each nation should have *"a right to the conditions necessary to the fulfillment of its national mission."*[26] This "mission" consists of the unique ideas and practices that it can add to the world's stock of ideas and techniques. Second, *"Any nation whose government in pursuit of a presumed national mission violates the conditions of community contradicts in action the very meaning of 'mission,' and thus undermines its own right."*[27] The basic condition of community requires each nation to respect every other as an end in itself and as a potential source of valuable experiments. Third, *"Each nation has not only a right but a duty to aim at world-power through the free spread of ideas."*[28] Each should attempt to extend its influence by winning respect for its own experiments. States which pursue this goal need not collide; as they learn from each other, their relations may be characterized by an "interpenetration" of cultural achievements and political practices.[29]

Although personal ethics can be applied to relations between states only through the concept of national experimentation, there is one situation in which Hocking thinks standards of personal morality should prevail. Toward the end of World War II and immediately afterward, he argued that Germany should not be punished, even though the moral indignation against her for initiating the war and for using genocidal methods was justified.[30] His study of wartorn Germany, the basis for *Experiment in Education*, convinced him even more strongly that a nation, even an aggressor, should be treated with forgiveness after its defeat. The attempt to punish a defeated nation is a denial of respect for its national experimentation. The crimes of a defeated government never justify the attempt to destroy "the permanent sources of national existence and fertility."[31] There are three

[25] *SWP*, pp. 186-87.
[26] *EE*, p. 211.
[27] *Ibid.*, p. 213.
[28] *Ibid.*, p. 215.
[29] *SMN*, p. 174.
[30] "On the Treatment of Germany," pp. 3-4.
[31] *EE*, p. 214.

other reasons why forgiveness is more appropriate than punishment. First, punishment of a nation makes everyone in that nation suffer, and in modern warfare all citizens are not equally guilty.[32] Second, warmaking is now so destructive that there is "no reparation, no suffering, no atonement" that can suffice as a punishment.[33] Aggressive war-making is a crime too great to be punished other than through defeat itself.[34] Third, there is no means of punishing a defeated nation that does not punish the punisher as well. It requires an expenditure of power to keep a defeated country powerless, and a nation that polices another must develop the psychology of the jailer.[35] What is necessary is the rebirth of the former enemy, the recovery of its self respect and its status in the world community.[36]

Hocking's general approach to ethics in international relations was the foundation for his analysis of specific issues and conflicts. Two positions that he developed over a period of time in a number of publications should be mentioned. After travels to the Near East in 1928 to study the British and French Mandates of Egypt, Syria and Palestine, he expressed an interest in the conditions of colonies dominated by Western powers.[37] He defended independence movements before it was popular to do so, because he thought all peoples had a right to experiment as well as a duty to share with the world their national uniqueness. The Western domination of non-Western nations was there-

[32] "The Treatment of Ex-Enemy Nations," p. 48.
[33] "On the Treatment of Germany," p. 3.
[34] *EE*, pp. 90-91.
[35] "On the Treatment of Germany," p. 3.
[36] "Death and Resurrection in the Life of Nations," *University of Chicago Round Table*, No. 367 (April 1, 1945), pp. 4-6. For his criticism of the American attempt to "re-educate" Germany see *EE*, pp. 40-107. He opposed American policy on two basic grounds. First, the "denazification" program of the Military Occupation forces wrongly tried to measure guilt presumptively on the basis of Nazi party affiliation and official rank. The Occupation should have tried instead to devise a method of determining present allegiance. Moreover, the punishments which were meted out to persons deemed most guilty consisted for the most part in "public demeanment" through the removal of various kinds of privileges. This, he thinks, did little either to change these people or to utilize their talents in building a new Germany. The second basic mistake was the failure to realize that the radical mental transformation of Germans which was desired could only be effected by the German people themselves. What the defeat of Germany could not do by way of a change in attitudes our own efforts could not achieve.
[37] In the report on his study, *The Spirit of World Politics*, he concluded that in their control of the "Class A" mandates of Palestine and Syria, Britain and France were not meeting the general requirements stipulated by the League Covenant for mandatory powers. Instead of accepting their responsibility to prepare the areas for self government, the European powers simply interpreted the mandate as a more decorous way than conquest to acquire territory formerly controlled by Germany and Turkey. See especially, Pts. I-V.

fore wrong in principle, he argued. Each nation should control its destiny as an independent state.[38]

After his trip to the Near East he also maintained an interest in the conflict between Arabs and Jews in Palestine. Only the general nature of his concerns can be mentioned. An evaluation of his arguments is outside the scope of his study, and it is really not fair to give great attention to a person's earlier views on a continuing political controversy, especially when we do not know how his position would have developed. Before the partition of Palestine and the establishment of the state of Israel in 1948, Hocking basically argued that it was not possible for one national "experiment in living" to receive political expression in that area without perpetuating the conflict. He thought Palestine should belong "to the universal culture,. . . to peace and understanding between races and religions."[39] The only alternative to conflict, he argued, was the maintenance of a bi-national home for both Jews and Palestinian Arabs. He thus did not accept the goal of "political Zionists," control of the political institutions of Palestine.[40] From 1948 to 1958 he wrote that the Arabs were not likely to accept as a *"fait accompli"* either Israel's enlargement of its borders or its policy toward the Palestinian refugees.[41] He argued that if a people deeply feels that it has been wronged, the passage of time will not necessarily bring acceptance of the new status quo.

SECURING INTERNATIONAL PEACE

Hocking always rejected both isolationism and a superficial internationalism. He supported American involvement in World War I,

[38] See *ibid.*, pp. 3-39, 196-224, 520-32, and "Colonies and Dependent Arears" (privately printed).
[39] "Misconceptions about Palestine," p. 932.
[40] Hocking wrote that "political Zionists" interpreted the British Balfour Declaration of 1917 to mean that Britain was committed to Jewish political control, to a Jewish state in Palestine. Other Jews, "cultural Zionists," took a more realistic view of the Declaration; they assumed the "National Home" was an area into which Jews could freely move to maintain their culture and worship. See *SWP*, pp. 335-92, and "Arab Nationalism and Political Zionism." Hocking quotes the Balfour Declaration (*SWP*, p. 372):
"'His majesty's Government view with favour the establishment in Palestine of a National Home for the Jewish people, and will use their best endeavours to facilitate the achievement of this object, it being clearly understood that nothing shall be done which may prejudice the civil and religious rights of existing non-Jewish communities in Palestine, or in the rights and political status enjoyed by Jews in any other country.'"
[41] See "When is a Fait Accompli?" (mimeographed); "Peace by Persuasion in the Middle East: An Analysis with Proposals for Solution of the Arab-Israeli Problem," (privately printed); and "Who Began the Israel-Arab War?" Letter to the editor of the *St. Louis Post Dispatch*, July 26, 1957, p. 2B.

and he argued strongly for American entry into the League of Nations.[42] But he never lapsed into that isolationist disillusionment that characterized so many liberals during the inter-war years.[43] He continued to support the principles of international organization and cooperative international action to secure peace. At the same time, his political philosophy led him to understand the strength of the political bonds within states and the role of states in the development of the potentialities of individuals. He therefore thought that a world government was not only impossible, but it was also not yet desirable.

During World War II he wrote a feature article in *Life* magazine, a forum that has been available to few other philosophers, in which he argued that the United States should not follow a neo-isolationist, "security-first" policy in the post-war years.[44] America should work instead to create a new international organization to replace the defunct League. In discussions concerning the proposed United Nations he was much more reluctant to sanction the use of force by an international organization against a power threatening peace than he was during and after World War I. In late 1915 he had stated that just as the good citizen has a responsibility to prevent not simply the burglary of his own house, but all house-breaking, so the United States has a responsibility for the "world's peace and lawful behavior."[45] In 1944 he expressly stated that such a breaking-and-entering analogy dismisses "too easily the deep roots of war" and evades "the world-wide responsibility for inquiry into the source of the trouble."[46]

He was also more reluctant to support the use of force by an international organization than he had been after the first World War. He realized that the employment of force to secure peace must be based on a wide consensus. "The appeal to force in advance of the development of a world opinion can only tend to disrupt the organization it-

[42] In the summer of 1916, at the age of 43, he volunteered for the Civilian's Military Training Camp at Plattsburg, New York, and during the next academic year he helped teach field surveying and map-making in the R.O.T.C. program at Harvard. During the summer of 1917 he was an observer on the French front for the British Department of Information, and he delivered speeches in England on the American commitment to the war. After the publication of *Morale and Its Enemies* in 1918, while continuing to hold teaching positions, he inspected "war-issues" courses for the War Department. For a full account of his experiences during this period and his reflections on them, see *Varieties of Educational Experience*, II, pp. 36-59.
[43] For a summary of American thought during this period, see Robert Endicott Osgood, *Ideals and Self Interest in America's Foreign Relations* (Chicago: University of Chicago Press, 1953), pp. 309-80.
[44] See "America's World Purpose."
[45] "Policing the World," letter to the editor of the *Springfield* (Mass.) *Republican*, December 15, 1915, p. 10.
[46] "Is a World Police Possible?" p. 1348.

self. For world force, apart from world confidence, is a nest of world suspicions."[47] The use of force against a great power would probably begin a war, and the use of force against smaller powers would only confirm the status quo of great power supremacy. During the planning of the United Nations, he supported the Soviet Union's argument that the great powers should have a veto on the Security Council. That proposal recognized, he wrote, the necessity of agreement among most states in the world, particularly among the great powers, before force is used.[48]

Hocking also recognized that a consensus must precede the development of any international law which could be significant in the maintenance of peace. The much used phrase, "world peace through world law," should be abandoned, since world law can only develop through world peace.[49] International law cannot be developed by the fiat of an international organization, he wrote; it must evolve through custom as states slowly find rules which preserve their mutual interests. "The acceptance of a common law is a consequence of living together, reaching empirical adjustments which become first custom, and then law."[50] He thought the development of an international consensus and standards of customary behavior would be furthered by the growth of a "world culture" or "world civilization." He argued that there is already a rudimentary world culture of science and technology, but higher levels of this culture depend on the growth of an "emotional unity" that is far more difficult to realize.[51] This emotional unity would be substantially furthered, he believed, by the evolution of a "world religion" or "world faith" as a center of loyalty and agreement among men. In *Living Religions and a World Faith* he studied the actual and potential interaction among existing major religions. This aspect of his thought lies outside the present study and has been treated admirably by others.[52]

[47] *Ibid.*, p. 1349.
[48] *Ibid.*, pp. 1348-49.
[49] "Footholds Toward Contest Without War," *U.S. Congressional Record*, CVIII, Part 8 (June 13, 1962), p. 10333.
[50] *SMN*, p. 181.
[51] *LRWF*, p. 265.
[52] See especially Rouner, *Within Human Experience*, *op. cit.*, pp. 256-310. The method of interaction between the world religions that Hocking thinks most fruitful for the development should be mentioned; it is discussed in *LRWF*, pp. 143-208. He suggests that the "way of reconception" is superior to the "way of radical displacement" or the "way of synthesis." The "way of radical displacement" is completely rejected. It insists that there is a special revelation from God specifying a particular set of beliefs which must be accepted if salvation is to be gained and eternal punishment or death is to be escaped. This approach was, he thinks, followed in Asia by those Christian missionaries who pulled converts from their local

During the years after World War II, Hocking considered the problem of maintaining international peace in the absence of a viable international law and an international organization that could effectively utilize force. He decided that a "creative diplomacy" is the only basis for peace. In 1959, before Cold War rhetoric was questioned by most American liberals, he published *Strength of Men and Nations*, subtitled, "*A Message to the USA vis-a-vis the USSR.*" It was, he admitted, a "pamphlet, a tract for the times," not a well-developed book.[53] Nevertheless, it does not yet seem entirely dated. He argues that American policy toward the Soviet Union has been too rigid and too little interested in discovering real bases of common agreement. The United States has wrongly considered the Soviet Union to be pure evil in substance and intention.[54] Of course, each nation has its "Defenders of the Faith" who cite fact and scripture to prove that the other is out to destroy it. National policy resting on such premises assumes that "we can do no less – and little more – than stand on guard and keep our nuclear press-buttons handy."[55] But such an assumption offers no hope for the development of understanding and trust between the two powers. It is therefore an unrealistic, vicious circle that may be escaped only through a creative diplomacy that avoids the stereotypes of previous policy.[56]

Hocking thinks the United States could initiate such a creative diplomacy by simply realizing that the Soviet Union and "socialist China" are here to stay.[57] It should attempt to understand that the

cultural traditions, thus aiding Western imperialistic efforts. The second approach, "synthesis," is followed when one religion indiscriminately adopts the beliefs of other religions without regard to consistency or to genuine disagreements between the two. The "way of reconception" is practiced when adherents of one religion "reconceive" their own religion and other religions in terms of their common "essence" or "generating principle." This "reconception" brings an increased awareness of the unity underlying the world religions. He advocates that a chain of centers be set up around the world where the members of the various religions may gather for conversation and for study of the relationship between the religion of that area and the surrounding culture. Thus, while Hocking is himself a Christian, he thinks that a "world faith" may develop which will include the "essence" of the existing world religions.

[53] *SMN*, p. 7.
[54] *Ibid.*, pp. 128-29.
[55] *Ibid.*, p. 129.
[56] *Ibid.*, pp. 137-42.
[57] Hocking thinks one example of the failure of the United States to achieve this realization is demonstrated in the confrontation on the islands of Quemoy and Matsu off the mainland coast of China. He argues that we should plan for "the normalization of the relations of the Chinese coast to the Chinese people." See "Containment as a Policy," letter to the editor of the *New York Times*, April 29, 1956, p. 8E. It is silly to believe that the defense of those islands is necessary to the security of Taiwan. Their only conceivable importance rests on Chaing Kaishek's impossible dream of reconquering the mainland: "To say that Taiwan itself is threatened by the proximity of Quemoy and Matsu in Mao's hands is to say that

Soviet Union has a genuine fear of the West. This fear exists partially because the system established by every victorious revolution has a defensive fear of condemnation from apologists for the destroyed regime.[58] Although its distrust is also partially based on the Marxist suspicion of capitalism, the most important reason for the Soviet fear stems from a general hostility to the makers of the Versailles treaty and the Munich pact.[59] In particular, Hocking believes the Soviet Union resents the Western attempt to place the blame for the beginning of World War II on Russia's participation in the Molotov-Ribbentrop Pact of 1939, an interpretation the United States continually defended.[60]

The United States should, Hocking writes, also be open to changes in the Soviet understanding of Marxist-Leninist ideology. Russian pronouncements about "peaceful co-existence" are sincere. Although this Soviet policy does not completely supplant the orthodox Marxist-Leninist dream of world revolution, it suggests "that a familiar process is taking place of transposing that dream from the realm of literal program to the realm of symbol, from a call to war to the guiding spirit of experimental challenge."[61] In a statement which Senator Clark inserted into the United States *Congressional Record*, Hocking points out that creative diplomacy should not approach ideologies in either of two common, but futile ways: "There are those who argue it out with the contrasting ideologies, as if they were the whole issue, easing the whole picture into an academic frame." There are also "those who deal solely with the gangs-and-methods, assuming the crimes of revolution inherent in the ideology, and condemning in advance anyone so much as lends an ear to the reprobate point of view."[62] Ideologies are not static, he writes; instead, they develop their own self-criticism as they are practiced. A creative diplomacy must be open to these changes.

One experiment in which every nation engages is the organization of

China is altogether too near Taiwan for comfort. So it is." See "Control if Islands," letter to the editor of the *New York Times*, September 10, 1958, p. 32.

[58] *SMN*, p. 132.

[59] *Ibid.*, p. 184.

[60] Hocking states that the Soviet Union firmly believes that it made the monaggression pact of 1939 only after its offer to stand with England and France in defense of Czechoslovakia was rebuffed by those powers. See *ibid.*, pp. 83-84. He reports that he was in Europe at the time of the Munich pact and that it was widely known that Stalin made such an offer and had even mobilized the Russian army along the border of Czechoslovakia. See "Interpreting Munich Era," letter to the editor of the *New York Times*, December 4, 1958, p. 38.

[61] *SMN*, p. 135.

[62] "Footholds Toward Contest Without War," p. 10332.

its economic life, and Hocking thinks it is possible for nations with differing economic systems to cooperate politically.[63] He rejects the argument that the differences between the Soviet and American economic systems are so great that neither can learn from the other: both have "mixed economies" to some degree, and there are some basic principles to which both subscribe.[64] Also, since a creative diplomacy values the "experiments in living" of other nations, the United States must move beyond the state of "denunciatory confront-ation," Hocking thinks. The nation that takes seriously the importance of other national experiments will neither attempt to impose its own experiments on them nor deny them the opportunity to make their experiments known. Therefore, he argues, the American "notion of throwing around the Western Hemisphere a cordon sanitaire from which Socialist ingredients are to be excluded becomes incongruous. Monroe Doctrines are not qualified to exclude ideas, or experiments with ideas."[65]

The adoption of a creative diplomacy would require an "announced abandonment of the pursuit of an infinitely retreating security."[66] It would also seek to establish conversation between citizens of the United States and the Soviet Union, even though any opening of conversation is a risk "based on nothing more than the certitude of the aboriginal democracy" between all men.[67] Such conversation would be encour-aged if the United States were to "open wide the channels of travel, trade, exchange of technique, science, and the temper of inquiry."[68] Personal relationships between officials of the two countries might also help to increase this mutual confidence, Hocking continues, especially if they took place outside the glare of publicity. Although such personal contact will not suddenly dissolve the differences between the two na-tions, it will help to increase the understanding and trust necessary for any genuine political settlement.[69]

Finally, a creative diplomacy will avoid that "moralizing" style

[63] "Private Property and Property Systems," p. 3; *SMN*, pp. 42-43.
[64] He writes (*SMN*, pp. 61-62) that the principles are:
 "No fixed over-all equality of reward, canceling incentive;
 No destitution within the reach of community aid;
 No extreme group inequalities of income, creating social chasms, and inviting function-less indulgence;
 No individual accumulation without corresponding responsibility."
[65] "Footholds Toward Contest Without War," p. 10333.
[66] *SMN*, p. 189.
[67] *Ibid.*, p. 196.
[68] *Ibid.*, p. 197.
[69] "Meeting with the Russians," letter to the editor of the *New York Times*, April 20, 1958, p. 8B. See also "Footholds Toward Contest Without War," p. 10333.

of diplomacy that appeals to "formulated principles rather than to the living feeling of justice in particular situations."[70] The morality that is creative and reconciling is "prior to general principle": it is the "morality of understanding and therefore of mental inclusiveness."[71] Although this morality provides only an indirect application of the standards of personal ethics to international affairs, Hocking realizes that it is the best hope for securing peace. Such a morality flows from the concept of national experimentation that Hocking develops. This concept of national experimentation shows what is required for the maintenance of that degree of liberty and community that is attainable in international relations: each state must freely pursue its own "experiment in living," and, at the same time, each must respect and try to learn from other national experiments.

[70] *SMN*, p. 233.
[71] *Ibid.*, p. 234.

CONCLUDING STATEMENT

Hocking offers an important, original political philosophy that is focused on theoretical problems related to the significant modern themes of liberty and community. It is the conclusion of this study that his political philosophy deserves much wider consideration than it has received. Because it is grounded in a comprehensive philosophical perspective, his political thought has great unity and depth. Those already familiar with Hocking will wish to examine the way his metaphysics and epistemology are applied to and influenced by his analysis of political matters. Because very little American political thought has been truly philosophical, students of political theory will be particularly interested in how Hocking, an American philosopher, discusses concepts important in the tradition of political philosophy. Social scientists will find that his theory offers both generalized insight into political problems and a heuristic source of more specific hypotheses. His political philosophy should also receive the attention of the broadly educated everywhere. For Hocking is, above all else, a philosopher of hope, and we are today very much in need of hope. In a 1963 *Saturday Review* article entitled "The Freedom to Hope," he wrote, "Faith that the future can be shaped is the core of action, and especially of human action." His political philosophy will help us to rethink those deterministic assumptions that undermine our sense of integrity and freedom, as well as those subjectivistic presuppositions that destroy our belief in the possibility of sociality and community.

Hocking's approach to the study of man, society, and the political community is philosophical. The contemporary social sciences have, however, largely patterned their study after the scientific method of the physical sciences. Confronted by this challenge, Hocking offers an important defense of political philosophy and other approaches that do not utilize the scientific method. The virtue of the scientific method, according to its proponents, is its exclusion of "values" from the process of investigation. Values are assumed to be mere "subjective preferences," and thus non-cognitive. Hocking correctly argues that this narrow empiricism should not be accepted as the sole valid approach to the study of man. Since it cannot grasp important dimensions of human experience, the scientific method will be destructive of both liberty and community if it is not supplemented by a "broadened empiricism." The widened empiricism that Hocking formulates is a personal and participatory style of inquiry. It insists that values, commitments, and emotions are integral to the dialectic of thought and experience and are cognitive in nature. Moreover, a broadened empiricism furthers the experience of freedom by accepting the cognitive status of all aspects of experience, and it strengthens community by stressing the dialectical, interpersonal nature of knowledge.

Hocking successfully formulates an "individualistic theory of society," a theory that allows for both individual autonomy and social unity. His theory is conceptually sound and adequately explains personal experience; the burden of proof rests on those who require another theory of man in society. He rejects those hereditary and environmental determinisms of contemporary social thought through his concept of the self as a "field of fields." And he explains that it would not make sense to discuss the self without presupposing its unity and purposiveness. He uses the concept of the "will to power" to show how the person's sense of identity and freedom develop as he fulfills his unique capacities. Hocking's theory also indicates that men are never completely imprisoned within the social structures of the past; social change is a constantly occurring process. Although neither conventions nor the generalized opinions of others can determine human thought and behavior, the individual requires social relations to develop his potentialities. The "will to power" flowers in a social context, not in isolation. Participation in the private and public orders of society is thus necessary to true individuality. Hocking's conception of these two orders is fundamental to his theory of the political community.

He extends his individualistic theory of society into an individualistic theory of the political community. It is a persuasive theory, grounded in his examination of those theoretical positions that question the dominant contemporary form of political organization. After rejecting the assumption that power is the essence of politics, he shows how the political community can achieve its purpose – the provision of conditions necessary to individual development. He uses the concept of the "will circuit" to explain how men can be politically united without losing their individuality: the state is a "coincident will circuit" that requires sovereignty to achieve its purpose; but its decisions and actions must be rooted in the shared commitments of its member individuals.

This individualistic theory of the political community maintains a tension between the individual's rights and his community responsibilities. Hocking's theory of rights provides a concept of political limits and a set of limits on the individual's claim to rights against the political community. He retains liberalism's traditional commitment to the uniqueness and inherent worth of the individual. But his reformulation of liberalism rejects the extreme individualism that leads to social disunity, the abandonment of the pursuit of excellence, and the separation of the claim of rights from the acceptance of political duty. He shows that true individualism is compatible with a healthy and vigorous political community. His approach to political participation also reconciles the political involvement of citizens with effective leadership. And his perspective on free expression balances the individual's right of expression with the requirements of community. Although he agrees with the conclusion that free expression is an important right, he demonstrates that liberalism's arguments for this conclusion should and can be strengthened.

Hocking's approach to international relations is analogous to his individualistic theory of society and the political community. It is individualistic in its insistence that each nation must pursue its own "experiment in living"; and it emphasizes that the degree of community possible in the relations between nations is achievable only if each respects and attempts to learn from the experiments of every other. This concept of the nation as an "experiment in living" is the foundation both for his perspective on the role of ethics in international relations and for his analysis of the problem of securing international peace. His last book is still relevant today: he persuasively argues that we must abandon the drive for security in favor of a "creative diplomacy" that can evoke mutual trust between nations.

In all his thought Hocking calls on men to reject the preoccupation with security in their personal and political lives in favor of an openness to the possibilities of change in individuals and institutions. Because it is oriented toward this openness, his political philosophy is dialectical, not dogmatic; yet, it is at the same time both comprehensive and consistent. It is grounded in his own experience, and he believes it will be corroborated in ours. Although this political philosophy offers no final answers to our specific practical problems, it will help us to think through that whole series of theoretical questions that are centered around the crucial contemporary concepts of liberty and community.

SELECTED BIBLIOGRAPHY OF WILLIAM ERNEST HOCKING

BOOKS

The Coming World Civilization. London: George Allen and Unwin, Ltd., 1958.

Experiment in Education: What we can Learn from Teaching Germany. Chicago: Henry Regnery Co., 1954.

Freedom of the Press: A Framework of Principle. Chicago: University of Chicago Press, 1947.

Human Nature and Its Remaking. New Haven: Yale University Press, 1918.

The Lasting Elements of Individualism. New Haven: Yale University Press, 1937.

Living Religions and a World Faith. New York: The Macmillan Co., 1940.

Man and the State. New Haven: Yale University Press, 1926.

The Meaning of God in Human Experience. New Haven: Yale University Press, 1912.

The Meaning of Immortality in Human Experience. New York: Harper and Brothers, 1957.

Morale and Its Enemies. New Haven: Yale University Press, 1918.

Preface to Philosophy: Textbook. New York: The Macmillan Company, 1946.

This book was written by Hocking and three others, Brand Blanshard, Charles W. Hendel, and John H. Randall, Jr. Each author's contribution is signed. Hocking is the author of Part I, "What is Man," pp. 3-99, and Part V, "A World-View," pp. 413-504.

The Present Status of the Philosophy of Law and of Rights. New Haven: Yale University Press, 1926.

Re-Thinking Missions. New York: Harper and Brothers, 1932.

Science and the Idea of God. Chapel Hill: The University of North Carolina Press, 1944.

The Self: Its Body and Freedom. New Haven: Yale University Press, 1928.

The Spirit of World Politics: With Special Studies of the Near East. New York: The Macmillan Co., 1932.

Strength of Men and Nations: A Message to the USA vis-a-vis the USSR. New York: Harper and Brothers, 1959.

Types of Philosophy. 3d ed. New York: Charles Scribner's Sons, 1959.

This edition was revised in collaboration with his son, Richard Boyle O'Reilly Hocking.

What Man Can Make of Man. New York: Harper and Brothers, 1942.

ARTICLES

"Action and Certainty." *Journal of Philosophy*, XXVII (April 24, 1930), 225-38.

"America Does Have Something of Offer the New Era." *Alumnus of Iowa State College*, XXXIX (April, 1944), 176-79.

"America's World Purpose." *Life*, April 17, 1944, pp. 103-04, 106, 109, 110, 112.

"Analogy and Scientific Method in Philosophy." *Journal of Philosophy, Psychology, and Scientific Methods*, VII (March 16, 1910), 161.

"Arab Nationalism and Political Zionism." *Moslem World*, XXXV (July, 1945), 216-23.

"The Atom as Moral Dictator." *Saturday Review of Literature*, February 2, 1946, pp. 7-9.

"The Binding Ingredients of Civilization." *Goethe and the Modern Age*. Edited by Arnold Bergstraesser. Chicago: Henry Regnery Co., 1950.

"Can Values be Taught?" *The Obligation of Universities to the Social Order* Edited by Henry P. Fairchild. New York: New York University Press, 1933.

"Christianity and Intercultural Contacts." *Journal of Religion*, XIII (April, 1934), 127-38.

"Conference on the Relation of Law to Social Ends." *Journal of Philosophy, Psychology, and Scientific Methods*, X (September 11, 1913,) 512-28.

"Conformity and Revolt." *The Smith Alumnae Quarterly* (August, 1936), pp. 338-41.

"Creating a School." *Atlantic Monthly*, December, 1955, pp. 63-66. This article was written in collaboration with his wife, Agnes Hocking.

"The Creed of Philosophical Anarchism." *Leviathan in Crisis*. Edited by Waldo R. Browne. New York: The Viking Press, 1946.

"Cross Currents in Asian Aims." *Asia*, XXXVI (April, 1936), 235-38.

"The Cultural and Religious Organization of the Future." *Toward International Organization*. No editor. New York: Harper and Brothers, 1942.

"Culture and Peace," "Faith and World Order," and "Statesmanship and Christianity." *The Church and the New World Mind*. No editor. St. Louis: The Bethany Press, 1944.

"Democracy and the Scientific Spirit." *American Journal of Ortho-Psychiatry*, X (July, 1940), 431-36.

"Dewey's Concepts of Experience and Nature." *Philosophical Review*, XLIX (March, 1940), 228-44.

"The Dilemma in the Conception of Instinct, as Applied to Human Psychology." *Journal of Abnormal and Social Psychology*, XVI (June-September, 1921), 73-96.

"The Diplomacy of Suspicion and the League of Nations." *University of California Chronicle*, XXI (April, 1919), 83-95.

"A Discussion of the Theory of International Relations." *Journal of Philosophy*, XLII (August 30, 1945), 484-86.

"Does Civilization *Still* Need Religion?" *Christendom*, I (October, 1935), 31-43.

"Dutch Higher Education – Comparative Impressions of a Visiting Harvard Professor." *Harvard Educational Review*, XX (Winter, 1950), 28-35.

"The Ethical Basis Underlying the Legal Right of Religious Liberty as Applied to Foreign Missions." *International Review of Missions*, XX (October, 1931), 493-511.

"Ethics and International Relations." *Journal of Philosophy, Psychology, and Scientific Methods*, XIV (December 6, 1917), 698-700.

"Fact and Destiny, I." *Review of Metaphysics*, IV (September, 1950), 1-12.

"Fact and Destiny, II." *Review of Metaphysics*, IV (March, 1951), 319-42.

"Fact, Field and Destiny: The Inductive Element in Metaphysics." *Review of Metaphysics*, XI (June, 1958), 525-49.

"Famine Over Bengal." *Asia*, XLIV (August, 1944), 345-49.

"The Finer Arts of Pugnacity." *The Spirit of Scholarship*. No editor. Greencastle, Indiana: DePauw University, 1940.

"Foreward." *The Arab World: Past, Present and Future*. Nejla Izzedin, author. Chicago: Henry Regnery Co., 1953.

"The Freedom to Hope." *Saturday Review*, June 22, 1963, pp. 12, 13-15, 50.

"The Function of Science in Shaping Philosophic Method." *Journal of Philosophy, Psychology, and Scientific Methods*, II (August 30, 1905), 477-86.

"The Future of Liberalism." *Journal of Philosophy*, XXXII (April 25, 1935), 230-47.

"The Group Concept in the Service of Philosophy." *Journal of Philosophy, Psychology, and Scientific Methods*, III (January 4, 1906), 5-12.

"Hard Facts in the East." *Asia*, XXXVI (April, 1936), 235-38.

"History and the Absolute." *Philosophy, Religion, and the Coming World Civilization*. Edited by Leroy S. Rouner. The Hague: Martinus Nijhoff, 1966.

"The Holt-Freudian Ethics and the Ethics of Royce." *Philosophical Review*, XXV (May, 1916), 479-506.

"How Can Our Schools Enrich the Spiritual Experience of Their Students?" *Beacon* (October, 1943), pp. 195-206.

"How Ideas Reach Reality." *Philosophical Review*, XIX (May, 1910), 302-18.

"Illicit Naturalizing of Religion." *Journal of Religion*, III (November, 1923), 561-99.

"The Influence of the Future on the Present." *Harvard Allumni Bulletin*, XXVII (April 9, 1925), 817-23.

"Instinct in Social Psychology." *Journal of Abnormal and Social Psychology*, XVIII (July-September, 1923), 153-66.

"Is a World Police Possible?" *Christian Century*, November 22, 1944, pp. 1347-49.

"Is Israel a 'Natural Ally'?" *Christian Century*, September 19, 1951, pp. 1072-74.

"Issues in Contemporary Philosophy of Law." *Harvard Law School Record* (March 5, 1947), pp. 1, 4.

"Justice, Law, and the Cases." *Interpretations of Modern Legal Philosophies*. Edited by Paul Sayre. New York: Oxford University Press, 1947.

"Leaders and Led." *Yale Review*, XIII (July, 1924), 625-41.

"Marcel and the Ground Issues of Metaphysics." *Philosophy and Phenomenological Research*, XIV (June, 1954), 439-69.

"The Meaning of Liberalism: An Essay in Definition." *Liberal Theology: An Appraisal*. Edited by David E. Roberts and Henry P. van Dusen. New York: Charles Scribner's Sons, 1942.

"The Meaning of the Life and Death of John F. Kennedy." *Current* (January, 1964), pp. 38-39.

"Meanings of Life." *Journal of Religion*, XVI (July, 1936), 253-83.

"Metaphysics: Its Function, Consequences, and Criteria." *Journal of Philosophy*, XLIII (July 4, 1946), 365-78.

"Misconceptions about Palestine." *Christian Century*, July 1, 1936, pp. 930-32.

"Missions in a Nationalist Orient." *Christian Century*, February 23, 1955, pp. 236-37.

"Morale." *Atlantic Monthly*, December, 1918, pp. 721-28.

"The Nature of Morale." *American Journal of Sociology*, XLVII (November, 1941), 302-20.

"A New East in a New World." *Fortune*, August, 1942, pp. 107-10, 119-20, 122, 124, 126, 131.

"The New Way of Thinking." *Colby Alumnus*, XXIX (July 15, 1950), 3-7.

"On Philosophical Synthesis." *Philosophy East and West*, II (1952), 1117-29.

"On Royce's Empiricism." *Journal of Philosophy*, LIII (February 2, 1956), 57-63.

"On the Law of History." *University of California Publications in Philosophy*, II (September 17, 1909), 45-65.

"On the Present Position of the Theory of Natural Right." *Library of the Tenth International Congress of Philosophy*. Edited by F. W. Beth and H. J. Pos. Vol. I. Amsterdam: North Holland Publishing Co., 1949.

"On the Treatment of Germany." *Christianity and Crisis*, May 29, 1944, pp. 3-4.

"Our Western Measuring Stick Carried East." *Asia*, XXXI (September, 1931), 554-59, 600-04.

"Palestine: An Impasse?" *Atlantic Monthly*, July, 1930, pp. 121-32.

"Philosophy – the Business of Everyman." *Journal of the American Association of University Women*, XXX (June, 1938), 221-17.

"Political Philosophy in Germany." *Journal of Philosophy*, XII (October 14, 1915), 584-86.

"A Positive Role for the United States." *Harvard Guardian*, VI (December, 1941), 15-18.

"Preview of the War That Mustn't Happen." *Town Hall*, VIII, No. 24 (1946), 1-2.

"Private Property and Property Systems." *Post War World*. New York: Commission on a Just and Durable Peace of the Federal Council of the Churches of Christ in America, 1945, p. 3.

"Problems of World Order in the Light of Recent Philosophical Discussion." *American Political Science Review*, XLVI (December, 1952), 1117-29.

"Reality in Christian History." *The Crozer Quarterly*, XIV (October, 1937), 274-83.

"Reconception Reconsidered." *Christian Century*, March 2, 1955, pp. 268-69.

"Religion and the Alleged Passing of Liberalism." *Advance*, CXXVI (May 3, 1934), 86-88.

"Religion in War-Time." *Atlantic Monthly*, September, 1918, pp. 376-87.

"Religion of the Future." *Religion and Modern Life*. No editor. New York: Charles Scribner's Sons, 1927.

"The Religious Function of State Universities." *University of California Chronicle*, X (October, 1908), 454-66.

"Response to Professor Krikorian's Discussion." *Journal of Philosophy*, LV (March 27, 1958), 274-80.

"Schweitzer's Outlook on History." *Albert Schweitzer's Realms*. Edited by A. A. Roback. Cambridge, Massachussetts: Sci-Art Publishers, 1962.

"Science in Its Relation to Value and Religion." *Rice Institute Pamphlet*, XXIX (April, 1942), 143-221.

"Social Censorship." *Outlook and Independent*, CLIII (December 11, 1929), 579.

"Some Second Principles." *Contemporary American Philosophy: Personal Statements*. Edited by George P. Adams and William P. Montague. Vol. I. New York: The Macmillan Co., 1930.

"Sovereignty and Moral Obligation." *International Journal of Ethics*, XXVIII (April, 1918), 314-26.

"The Spiritual Effect of Warlessness." *A Warless World*. Edited by Arthur Larson. New York: McGraw-Hill Book Co., 1963.

"Theory of Value and Conscience in Their Biological Context." *Psychological Bulletin*, V (May 15, 1908), 129-43.

"Theses Establishing an Idealistic Metaphysics by a New Route." *Journal of Philosophy*, XXXVIII (December 4, 1941), 688-90.

"This is My Faith." *This is My Faith*. Edited by Stewart G. Cole. New York: Harper and Brothers, 1956.

"The Treatment of Ex-Enemy Nations." *Christianity Takes a Stand: an Approach to the Issues of Today*. Edited by William Scarlett. New York: Penguin Books, Inc., 1946.

"The War Zone and What Lies Behind It." *Harvard Alumni Bulletin*, XX (February 28, 1918), 411-14.

"Ways of Thinking About Rights: A New Theory of the Relation Between Law and Morals." *Law: A Century of Progress, 1835-1935*. No editor. Vol. II. New York: New York University Press, 1937.

"What Does Philosophy Say?" *Philosophical Review*, XXXVII (March, 1928), 133-53.

"The Working of the Mandates." *Yale Review*, XIX (December, 1929), 244-68.

LETTERS TO THE EDITOR*

"Analyzing German Reactions." *New York Times*, February 21, 1953, p. 12.

"Answer to a Threat." *New York Times*, October 25, 1920, p. 14.

"Arab World's Alienation Seen." *New York Times*, June 18, 1951, p. 22.

"Containment as a Policy." *New York Times*, April 29, 1956, p. 8E.

"Control of Islands." *New York Times*, September 10, 1958, p. 32.

"Finest Event." *New Hampshire Morning Union*, June 15, 1950, p. 4.

"Human Rights and Society." *Science*, CXXVIII (December 12, 1958), 1476.

"Informing the Armed Forces." *New York Times*, May 24, 1951, p. 34.

"Interpreting Munich Era." *New York Times*, December 4, 1958, p. 38.

"The Korean War: Current Defeatism Called Unjustified." (With others.) *New York Herald Tribune*, November 25, 1951, Sec. 2, p. 4.

"Lattimore, 'Patriot.' " *New Hampshire Morning Union*, August 19, 1950, p. 4.

"Meeting with the Russians." *New York Times*, April 20, 1958, p. 8B.

"Plan is Opposed as Source of Dissension." *New York Times*, April 2, 1944, Sec. 4, p. 8E.

"Policing the World." *Springfield [Mass.] Republican*, December 15, 1915, p. 10.

"Position of Ex-Nazis." *New York Times*, December 15, 1952, p. 12.

"Public's Stake in Steel." *New York Times*, May 10, 1959, Sec. IV, p. 10.

"A Reply to Dr. Stafford." *Advance*, September 3, 1951, p. 18.

"Who Began the Israel-Arab War?" *St. Louis Post Dispatch*, July 26, 1957, p. 2B.

BOOK REVIEWS

Review of *The Individual and the Social Order*, by Joseph A. Leighton. *Philosophical Review*, XXVII (September, 1928), 513-16.

Review of *The Political Theories of Martin Luther*, by Luther Hess Waring. *Yale Review*, XIX (February, 1911), 444-45.

Review of *The Public and Its Problems*, by John Dewey. *Journal of Philosophy*, XXVI (June 6, 1929), 329-35.

Review of *Religion as Man's Protest Against the Meaningless of Events*, by Martin P. Nilsson. *Review of Religion*, XIX (October, 1955), 83-87.

Review of *Social Organization*, by Charles Horton Cooley. *Yale Review*, XVIII (February, 1910), 420-22.

Review of *Tomorrow's Business*, by Beardsley Ruml. *Christian Science Monitor*, February 20, 1945, p. 16.

---

* Although the titles of these letters were generally given by the editor rather than by Hocking, they are included in order to clarify the nature of the letters.

TRANSCRIPTS OF RADIO AND TELEVISION DISCUSSIONS

"The Atom and World Politics." *University of Chicago Round Table*, No. 393 (September 30, 1945), 1-11.
Other participants in this radio discussion were Norman Cousins, William Fox, and Leo Szilard.
"The Crisis of Our Time." *University of Chicago Round Table*, No. 353 (December 24, 1944), 1-17.
Other participants in this radio discussion were Robert Hutchins, Reinhold Niebuhr, and Robert Redfield.
"Death and Resurrection in the Life of Nations." *University of Chicago Round Table*, No. 367 (April 1, 1945), 4-6.
Other participants in this radio discussion were Charles Merriam, Reinhold Niebuhr, and Robert Redfield.
"The Near East." *University of Chicago Round Table*, No. 224 (June 28, 1942), 2-14.
Other participants in this radio discussion were H. A. R. Gibb and Philip Ireland.
"The State of the Nation." *University of Chicago Round Table*, No. 406 (December 30, 1945), 4-7.
Other participants in this radio discussion were Ernest C. Colwell, T. R. Hogness, Reinhold Niebuhr, and Robert Redfield.
"What Price Victory?" *America's Town Meeting of the Air*, Vol. VIII, No. 20 (1942), 1-18.
Other participants in this radio discussion were Crane Brinton, Alvin H. Hansen, and Thomas Matters.
"Wisdom for Our Time." *Wisdom for Our Time*. Edited by James Nelson. New York: Norton and Co., Inc., 1961.
This is the transcript of an interview for television by the National Broadcasting Corporation.

GOVERNMENT DOCUMENTS

"Footholds Toward Contest Without War." *U. S. Congressional Record*, CVIII, Part 8 (June 13, 1962), 10332-34.
"A Philosophy of Life for the American Farmer and Others." *Farmers in a Changing World; The Yearbook of Agriculture, 1940*. Edited by Gove Hambidge. Washington: United States Government Printing Office, 1940, pp. 1056-71.

PUBLISHED ADDRESSES

"American Democracy: Traditional Defense, Actual Working." *Town Hall*, VIII (June 17, 1946).
This address is paraphrased by the editors; quotations should not be directly attributed to Hocking.
"Freedom of the Press in America." Leiden, Netherlands: Universitaire Pers Leiden, 1947.
"Immanuel Kant and International Policies." *Annual Report of the Directors of the American Peace Society*, XCVI (May, 1924), 19-28.

PRIVATELY PRINTED MATERIAL

"Colonies and Dependent Areas." Boston, Mass.: Universities Committee on Post-War International Problems, 1943.

"Peace by Persuasion in the Middle East: An Analysis with Proposals for Solution of the Arab-Israeli Problem." Edited by Virginia C. Gildersleeve. Distributed by the American Friends of the Middle East, 1958.

UNPUBLISHED MATERIAL

"Ethical Factors in Positive Law." Munich: 1948. (Mimeographed.)

"God and the Modern World." 1960. (Mimeographed.)

"Principles of Mass Communications by Radio and Television from the Angle of Philosophy and Psychology." 1959. (Mimeographed.)

Varieties of Educational Experience. Part I (1952) and Part II (1954). (Mimeographed.)

"When is a Fait Accompli?" 1957. (Mimeographed.)

INDEX

INDEX